Prophecy

GOD'S
POSITIONING SYSTEM
FOR OUR LIVES

"A new heart will I give you,
and a new spirit will I put within you;
and I will take away the stony heart
out of your flesh give you a heart of flesh."

Ezekiel 36:26 (AMPC)

ROSAMOND PANZARELLA

Prophecy: God's Positioning System for Our Lives
Trilogy Christian Publishers A Wholly Owned Subsidary of Trinity
Broadcasting Network
2442 Michelle Drive Tustin, CA 92780
Cover design by: Kelly Stewart
For information about special discounts for bulk purchases, please contact
Trilogy Christian Publishing.
Trilogy Disclaimer: The views and content expressed in this book are those
of the author and may not necessarily reflect the views and doctrine of Trilogy
Christian Publishing or the Trinity Broadcasting Network.
Manufactured in the United States of America
10 9 8 7 6 5 4 3 2 1
Library of Congress Cataloging-in-Publication Data is available.
ISBN: 979-8-88738-037-7
E-ISBN: 979-8-88738-038-4

DEDICATION

This book is dedicated to my wonderful husband, who has endless patience and a never-ending sense of humor. John, you make us all laugh. You are the family's "fix-it man." If you do not know how to fix something, you always say, "I will figure it out." You are also my confidant and counselor. You listen to my every concern and keep me balanced.

I also dedicate this book to our three lovely daughters:
Danyette Heine,
Jenny Burr, and
Shelley Panzarella.

May we all know and serve the Lord.

ACKNOWLEDGMENTS

A special appreciation to my wonderful friend, Susan Moore, who read my manuscript and offered suggestions and recommendations. Susan freely gave of her time, and I treasured her input and advice. Susan, you are an encouragement and a blessing to me and to many, many others.

TABLE OF CONTENTS

PREFACE

God has a purpose and a plan for everyone. Scripture underscores this fact because Jeremiah 29:11 (AMPC) says, *"For I know the thoughts and plans that I have for you, says the Lord, thoughts and plans for welfare and peace and not for evil, to give you hope in your final outcome."* At times, God's plan for our lives can be difficult to discern as we progress through life. A scripture that highlights this fact is Proverbs 20:24 (AMPC), which says, *"Man's steps are ordered by the Lord; how can a man then understand his way?"* This scripture makes the point that we might not always understand where God is directing our steps or know what we are supposed to do for the kingdom of God, but behind the scenes, God is directing our steps.

God has multiple ways to bring into fruition His plans for our lives. God may direct our path through dreams. There are numerous examples in the Bible where God used dreams to direct, instruct, and change biblical characters' plans. A well-known Bible story is when an angel appeared to Joseph in a dream. This angel directed Joseph to take Mary and baby Jesus and go to Egypt because of Herod's edict to kill all male babies two years old and younger. Then, when it was safe to return, God gave Joseph another dream. In this dream the angel appeared to Joseph, informing him it was now safe to return to Israel.

God may steer our path by using His Word. When reading the Bible, the Holy Spirit may alert us to pay attention to a specific scripture or a Bible story or a biblical passage with the Holy Spirit illuminating a passage in a special way. Somehow the Holy Spirit "lights up" a scripture to us; this is the Holy Spirit working in our hearts!

God may steer our path by impressing upon our hearts some keen insight, discernment, or an understanding about a situation or a matter. Kris Vallotton, in his book *Basic Training for the Prophetic Ministry*, said, "*At times, the Lord speaks to us in a still, small voice from within our spirit. This can be heard as a passing thought, a sudden impression, or an internal sense of something God is saying*" (Vallotton 2005, 43). In his book Vallotton cites the story about Elijah in the cave when the Lord passed by him. The Lord was not in the strong wind or an earthquake or a fire but in a gentle stillness (1 Kings 19:11–13). We can train ourselves to hear this still, small voice by getting quiet and taking the time to listen so that we do catch those spiritual impressions.

God may use prophetic words to "plant seeds" in our hearts. These prophetic words are desires God wishes to fulfill in a person's life. In his book *Prophets and Personal Prophesy*, Dr. Hamon said:

> *God plants within us a Kingdom seed, a vision, a divinely inspired ministry or project. He causes it to grow without much notice to others, or even to ourselves...nothing supernatural seems to be happening...But suddenly, when it has reached full maturity, when the person, the ministry, and God's purpose are ready, then immediately God harvests it by bringing it into full activity and fulfillment.*

Hamon 1993, 121

God may steer our path by using prophecy. In the Old Testament, in Numbers 11:17–29, prophecy is mentioned. In this passage the Lord told Moses to gather seventy elders and bring them to the tent of meeting so that He could distribute the Spirit that was upon Moses onto these selected leaders so they could share the burden of governing the people. Numbers 11:25 (AMPC) says, "*And the Lord came down in the cloud and spoke to him [Moses], and took of the Spirit that was upon him and put it upon the seventy elders; and when the Spirit rested upon them, they prophesied [sounding forth the praises of God and declaring His will].*" Then, Numbers 11:26 (AMPC) says, "*But there remained two men in the camp, named Eldad and Medad. The Spirit rested upon them, and they were of those who were selected and listed, yet they did not go out to the Tent [as told to do], but they prophesied in the camp.*" Then, in Numbers 11:27, a young man, concerned, ran to Moses, informing him that Eldad and Medad were prophesying in the camp. Joshua, in Numbers 11:28 (AMPC), alarmed, said to Moses, "*My lord Moses, forbid them!*" However, Moses replied in Numbers 11:29 (AMPC), "*Are you envious or jealous for my sake? Would that all the Lord's people were prophets, and that the Lord would put His Spirit upon them!*" So in the Old Testament, we find scripture that reveals that Moses valued prophecy.

Prophecy is also discussed in the New Testament. In 1 Corinthians 14:1 (NIV), Paul, writing about the spiritual gifts, said, "*Follow the way of love and eagerly desire the gifts of the spirit, especially prophecy.*" Paul then discussed in 1 Corinthians 14:3 (NIV) the purpose of prophecy, stating, "*But the one who prophesies speaks to people for edification strengthening, encouraging and comfort.*" Paul went on to say that edification instructs, educates, or "tutors" us, helping to promote spiritual growth. Comfort offers us spiritual support. Thus, prophetic words bring forth an assurance of love, support, and hope to the hearer. Paul encouraged prophecy in the churches at that time.

Today, some feel that the gifts of the Spirit, including prophecy, are no longer active. However, in my life the Lord has repeatedly demonstrated to me that this just is not true. There have been times when a prophetic word has absolutely "read my mail." I remember a prophetic word spoken to me during a Wednesday evening church service. At that time I was teaching a Bible history class as an elective course at the high school. You might think that students who signed up for a Bible history class would be angels in the classroom, but in this class, that was not the case. The prophetic word spoken to me that evening informed me that two to three students were making negative comments in class under their breath about me. In this prophetic word, I was informed that the Lord would deal with those students. However, I am getting ahead of my story.

Personal prophecy has a purpose in the church and in our lives today. I would like to take you on a journey, my journey, to share with you how personal prophecy has played a significant role in my life. In fact, I am writing this book out of obedience to a prophetic word spoken to me at a Christian conference in Houston. This prophetic word said:

> "'There have been some words that you have felt in your spirit. There have even been thoughts that you desire writing—even your own book,' says the Lord. The Lord says, 'I've birthed that idea within you... And other ministers are going to read that book and learn from it.' 'It is even going to cause them to even move in the direction that I have called them to because of you,' says God. So, you see, you are not one to seek or cause influence, but God says, 'I am calling you to be an influencer of influencers, and it is because you have not sought it on your own.' 'You first sought My face,' says God."

I can assure you that the Lord had to "birth within me" an idea to write a book. This was not on my "to-do list."

I hope in reading this book that pastors and individuals will gain greater insight into how the Lord uses personal prophecy to instruct and direct a person's life.

MY JONAH MOMENT

Sometimes the Lord calls you to do things you do not want to do. In the Old Testament, the Lord called Jonah to preach to the Ninevites, which Jonah was very reluctant to do. The Lord's instruction to Jonah was given with the command in Jonah 1:2 (AMPC), *"Arise, go to Nineveh, that great city, and proclaim against it, for their wickedness has come up before Me."* Not wanting to preach to the Ninevites nor follow through on the assignment the Lord had given him, Jonah ran away and headed for a ship bound for far-away Tarshish.

Buddy Scott, in one of his weekly columns in our local newspaper, *The Facts*, wrote about Jonah and stated, *"Rather than obeying God and spreading revival fires among the Ninevites, Jonah booked a passage on a ship and sailed away from God and his missionary assignment."*

I can certainly relate to Jonah's initial reaction of wanting to run away from a God-given assignment because I, too, momentarily experienced a "Jonah moment." My "Jonah moment" occurred on September

12, 2019, when I attended Life International Church's conference in Houston, Texas. At this conference, a prophetic word spoken to me stated that the Lord had birthed within me a desire to write a book. As I was receiving this word, I am sure I had the most incredulous look of unbelief on my face. I slowly moved my head from left to right several times as those words were spoken over me. This reaction was not out of rebellion on my part; it was just honest disbelief! I was shocked that the Lord was calling *me* to write a book!

Needless to say, I did not book a passage on a ship and run away like Jonah, but the next day when I was discussing this new assignment with my friend, Susan Moore, I became upset just talking about it. However, as I mentally processed this prophetic word over the next several days, I recovered from my initial shock and accepted the Lord's new assignment. So, following Abraham's example of obediently packing up his family, along with his nephew Lot, and walking out God's plan for his life, I obediently sat down at the computer, pondered my thoughts, planned my main points, and then began typing out topics and details for this new assignment—the book the Lord called *me* to write.

The only connection I have ever had concerning a book writing project was with my friend, Sandra Moraw

Sommerfrucht. In a conversation with me several years ago, Sandra declared, "I just feel like I could write a book!" She had this stirring in her heart to write a book, and she also has a natural flair for writing. This desire in Sandra's heart eventually manifested into a book titled *The Best Seat in the House*. This title relates to our "best seat," which is in Christ. After completing the book, Sandra asked me to read the manuscript, make comments, and even edit if anything caught my attention. That was a new experience for me. I had never read a book for that purpose. Several years later, Sandra authored a second book titled *How to Meet and Marry Your Covenant Mate*. This was a book about God's divine connections at work in our lives and how the Lord directed Sandra's steps to meet her husband, Jim. With the second book, Sandra asked me to write a recommendation to inform others how her book could perhaps benefit them.

Recently, I had a phone conversation with Sandra, and she said that she is now writing her third book. This book's theme is to show how God is a personal God caring about every detail of our lives because He loves us so much. In another phone conversation, Sandra informed me that she had finished writing her book, and a publisher had accepted her book for publication.

Concerning my book writing assignment, the Lord gave me four specific directives. He said to write about:

- all those things I went through,

- all those areas where I experienced growth,

- all those areas where I walked through the flames, and

- all those things in the area of ministry others would love to hear about.

When Sandra was writing her first book, I said to myself, *I'm sure glad writing a book is not one of my God-given assignments.*

Well...now it is!

Chapter One

ALL THOSE THINGS
I WENT THROUGH

THE EARLY YEARS

"Fear not [there is nothing to fear], for I am with you...I will strengthen and harden you to difficulties, yes, I will help you; yes, I will hold you up and retain you with My [victorious] right hand of rightness and justice."

Isaiah 41:10 (AMPC)

Most everyone has memories of an event in their life when they were very young. I remember listening to Dr. Dobson on his radio program one day as he shared his earliest childhood memory with his radio audience. His recollection centered on when he was just three years old, and he walked down the aisle of the church to give his heart to Jesus. That is a wonderful remembrance at such a young age. Reflecting on my own life, I realized my earliest childhood memory was when I was around the age of four. My recollection centers on my brother, who had the habit of sucking his thumb. We are only fourteen months apart in age, so he was probably around the age of five or so at that time. I watched as he secretively took the liquid bottle of "medicine" that our parents were using to try to prevent his thumb-sucking habit and hid it under the foundation of the house. At that time we lived in a house that was supported by cinder blocks, so this was an easy task for him to do. Needless to say, our parents never found the bottle of "medicine," and my brother continued his thumb-sucking habit. In fact, he continued this habit until he was in the second or third grade. Later, he told me that one day, he held up his thumb, looked at it, and said, "You know what, I don't need you anymore!" And that was the end of his thumb-sucking habit.

When we were very young, our parents were not home very much, and my brother and I lacked consistent parental supervision or any type of parental guidance. Both of our parents worked, which is not unusual, but some of their jobs had irregular hours, including working at night. My brother and I were frequently left alone—day and night. My father later told me there were times when he was not sure if there would even be money for a loaf of bread.

My brother was always looking for action, and

because of this fact, he would sometimes get into trouble. He had what I call his "wandering excursions" in the neighborhood. He would leave our duplex to "wander," and I would accompany him. My fear of staying home alone in the duplex when I was at that age was stronger than my fear of going with him and possibly getting into mischief or some type of trouble on these "outings." I do remember one evening the lady who was adjacent to our duplex came over and helped us get into our pajamas. I assume she stayed with us for a while because of the late hour; I just do not remember how long she stayed.

One day, my brother found some money tucked away in our parent's chest of drawers. He took the money, went to the small neighborhood grocery store nearby, and bought candy, which he freely passed out to kids in the neighborhood. Naturally, when our father found out what had happened, he was angry with my brother. My father took my brother to the small neighborhood grocery store where the candy had been purchased and confronted the store owner. Tagging along, I remember the store owner saying, "How was I supposed to know anything!" My father told the store owner not to ever sell anything else to my brother! Later, when I was older, my father told me that the money had been set aside to pay for the car insurance.

In a recent phone conversation with my brother, he said he remembered taking dollar bills and putting them on top of trash cans. He added, "You know money at that age doesn't mean anything to a kid." I do remember a lady bringing some dollar bills to my mother. Evidently, she had heard about the free-spending neighborhood boy and knew exactly where to return this "floating" money.

On another occasion when we were alone, our mother told us she would be home at twelve o'clock. So, we were two kids—left alone. When you are young, time seems to move very slowly. After a while, we became restless and wanted to know the time. Even a short amount of time seems like a long time at that age. So, we began knocking on neighbors' doors, asking them how soon before it would be twelve o'clock. Evidently, twelve o'clock noon had already passed for that day because we kept receiving the same reply over and over, "Tonight at twelve o'clock midnight." We became frustrated because that was not the answer we wanted to hear. I do not remember when our mother finally did come home; I just remember we became very exasperated at hearing the same answer every time, "Tonight at twelve o'clock midnight."

As I said, my brother was constantly looking for action, and if he did not find any, he created it. One time he took a large bucket outside our backdoor and stuffed it with newspapers and then lit the newspapers with a match. Thank goodness nothing caught on fire, and the fire died out. However, my brother also engaged in several experiments. On that day, he took some eggs, wrapped them in a blanket, put them in the oven, and turned it on. I assume he thought he could hatch some baby chicks. This idea did not work out too well. The kitchen became rather smoky. On another day, he decided to be the "chef for the day" and cook a chicken. He put a whole chicken in a pot, placed it on the oven rack, and turned on the oven, thinking he would produce a delicious meal. The outcome, however, was a very crisp, leathery piece of chicken. Thank goodness nothing dreadful happened with these experiments. We were just two young children who were home alone without parental supervision!

THE HOME ATMOSPHERE

I have only one memory of Christmas with the four of us as a family. At that time I was about six years old, and my brother was seven. On that Christmas morning, my brother and I opened our gifts—alone. I remember opening a gift, turning, and walking into our parent's bedroom to show them my present. What was their reaction? They both just ignored me, turned over in bed, and continued sleeping.

Also, the home atmosphere was anything but peaceful; in fact, it was chaotic! My parents constantly yelled at each other. They were always fighting. There was never any peace. With all the strife in our family, they eventually divorced.

At that time in society, judges and the court system placed children in the mother's care. So when the divorce was finalized, we were placed under our mother's supervision. Much, much later in life, I received a prophetic word that I blamed myself for my parent's divorce because I thought I had done something to cause it. I have read articles about the psychological impact of divorce on children. Divorce affects children no matter what age. Until that prophetic word was spoken to me, I did not realize that subconsciously I blamed myself for our parent's divorce. Often, we do not realize what heart issues need healing in our hearts because of circumstances and situations we have experienced in life.

After our parent's divorce, my mother, brother, and I moved to a different location. My brother and I were left alone—a lot. Since we were free to make our own choices, one hot summer day, we decided to see a movie, a scary movie. Why we chose a scary movie I do not know, but I am sure my brother had something to do with that decision. Six- and seven-year-olds should not see a scary movie because, at that young age, it is difficult to distinguish fantasy from reality. I do not even remember how we had the money to go to the movie, but by the time the movie was over, we were scared! Walking home at dusk, we became even more frightened. To distract ourselves, we began singing— loudly! Arriving at our apartment, my *big, older* brother made *me* step inside the front door and fumble for the light switch. I guess because he was my big, bossy brother, I did not argue with him. I hesitantly reached to the right of the door and, groping in the dark room, found the light switch, and I quickly flipped on the light. Recently I had a phone conversation with my brother and asked him if he remembered our going to the scary movie and the light switch incident. He answered, "Yes, and now I feel really bad about it." (Our perspective about situations in life changes as we age.)

I do not remember my brother and me ever sitting down to a family meal. I do recall, however, one special meal. An elderly husband and wife invited us to their home for supper. I am sure we met this couple because of my brother, who is a real talker; he would talk to anybody and everybody—anywhere. It did not matter whom my brother talked to; he never met a stranger. Even to this day, he is still a talker! However, on that day this caring couple served a hot meal, which was a real treat to us. I think, if my memory is correct, they invited us to eat twice with them. I am sure the Lord blessed this couple for feeding two young vagabonds who were forever wandering the neighborhood and who did not know what it was like to sit down and have a hot family meal with a mother and father.

About this time our mother moved the three of us to another apartment, which was near the downtown area of Montgomery, Alabama. Our apartment was upstairs. As usual, my brother created some type of action. One day, my brother placed a radio on the window ledge, so the sound projected directly outside. Just under the window was the yard man who was getting ready to cut grass for the apartment. My brother asked the man what type of music he liked. Receiving a reply, my brother proceeded to find a radio station to fit his request. Next, my brother turned the radio volume up to a loud blast so the yardman would be entertained while he worked. The neighbors were rather upset and complained to the apartment owner.

On another occasion I remember when a visitor, a

social worker, came to talk to our mother. I was with my mother in the backyard as she hung clothes on a clothesline. The social worker talked to her for quite some time and then left. Someone in the neighborhood or someone in our apartment evidently had complained to the social service department, whether it was due to the loud radio incident or the free-roaming children or perhaps all the noise we made upstairs when we were alone all day. Nothing came out of the social worker's visit; however, I do remember after the social worker left, our mother began walking up and down the block knocking on doors to see if there were any rooms for rent. Looking back, I realize that our mother planned to move because of all the complaints she received about her two nomadic children.

As I have said, our mother was not home very much. She worked as a waitress and had erratic hours, even working on Sundays. Sunday was the most boring day of the week for my brother and me because our playmates and their families went to church. So one Sunday, my brother and I decided we would go to church too. I do not remember how we found the church, but it must have been close to where we lived because we walked. I do not even remember if the walk was long or short; I just remember we walked to church. I do not remember much about the church visit or what we did, but I do have one poignant memory. I remember a man sitting behind a desk, conversing with us. I do not recall the length of the conversation. However, in his large office, I clearly remember this man commenting to us as we were leaving his office, "Well, bring your mother next time." As young as I was, I knew in my heart that this man really did not mean what he said. It should have seemed strange to him, or anyone for that matter, for a six-year-old and a seven-year-old to walk and attend church alone! The man just said, "Well, bring your mother next time."

One day during those summer months, our mother announced to us that we were going on a trip. To me at that age, that was exciting news! The next morning, I rose early. I remember watching dawn break over the horizon as I sat at the end of my mother's bed, waiting, anticipating a trip, and wanting her to get up and get ready. We were going somewhere! My brother, mother, and I traveled by bus on that day; the purpose of the trip was to visit an orphanage. My mother was searching for an orphanage that would accept my brother and me. This orphanage had many large buildings. We were escorted to two specific ones: the boy's dormitory and the girl's dormitory. I do not remember many other details about that day. I think, legally, our mother could not place us in this orphanage without our father's permission or his signature on the legal papers. So the outcome of this trip: our mother looked, and then we took a bus ride back to our apartment.

On one of those summer days, my brother had an argument with our mother. After arguing back and forth for a while, my brother then vehemently told our mother, "I'm leaving," and he did! My brother was seven years old! He left and walked to a busy downtown area of Montgomery, Alabama, where our father worked. We lived fairly close to the downtown area, so it was not an insurmountable feat, but it was quite a distance to walk. However, can you imagine a young boy walking all the way into town—alone! At the end of the workday, my father returned with my brother to our apartment. Our father told our mother that if she did not want to take care of us, he would. My mother, however, refused to consider that option.

Before those summer days ended, we went on another trip. This time our destination was a large two-story structure that sat at the top of a massive hill. To arrive at this place, we had to follow a long winding path that went around and around, and eventually, we came to the top of the hill. There sat a very large, two-storied spacious home—another orphanage. My mother's boyfriend had driven my mother, my brother, and me in his truck. After following the curvy path, my mother's boyfriend stopped the truck several hundred feet away from the front door, and he waited in his truck. Then, my mother, my brother, and I walked to the front door of this orphanage. We were greeted and ushered into a large living room area, and we sat down on one of several sofas in the room. Our mother talked to the husband-and-wife team, the overseers of the orphanage. After some discussion, they agreed to take us in even though my mother did not have any legal papers. This became our new home. Later, my father told me that our mother knew he was out of town on that weekend, so she was sure he could not interfere with her plans.

My brother, on the other hand, had other ideas about staying at the orphanage. Before the end of the first day, he ran away! It is amazing to me that a seven-year-old could walk all the way down this long winding hill to the main road; the main road was not just a small lane road but a busy road. He crossed the road and continued his "mission." I guess my brother could be compared to a pet that had been transported to a new home but decided to return to the old residence. My brother had a friend whom he had played with where we had lived, so I can only assume that was the fact that compelled him to leave the orphanage. I do not know how he managed to do it, but he walked a long, long way to return to his point of origination—our old apartment. When my brother was near the vicinity of where we had lived, he called our mother. She, in turn, immediately called the husband-and-wife team in charge of the orphanage. The husband came and picked my brother up. According to my brother, the man was not too happy with him, and he had to listen to a lecture all the way back to the orphanage.

THE ORPHANAGE

The orphanage cared for children and teenagers of all ages; however, I do not ever remember seeing babies there. It was understood by everyone that when you reached the age of eighteen and graduated from high school, you were then sent out into the world on your own. Everyone had assigned jobs, no matter what age. I guess because of my young age, I was assigned to clean the half-bath downstairs. I made sure I did my job and did not skip this assignment because I did not want to get into trouble. I probably had other jobs, but the downstairs half-bath is the only job I remember being assigned to do.

Because I made good grades in elementary school, I was given the privilege of taking piano lessons. This was a standard rule at the orphanage. There were several other girls who also took piano lessons with me. Since there was just one piano, we were given a specific time to practice our lessons each day. No one had to remind me to practice; I just did it. I was always obedient and wanted to do the right thing. Although it was a privilege to take piano lessons, I cannot say the experience was a delightful one. The piano teacher was not encouraging, nor did she show any compassion. In fact, she would take her long pointer stick, whose purpose was to point to the musical notes, and use the pointer stick to strike across my fingers whenever I made a mistake, hit a wrong note, or did something she did not like. Often, I wound up in tears during those sessions. This type of correction went on the whole time I took lessons from the piano teacher.

I also have memories concerning the girl's dormitory. One evening, we were just being typical kids, playing and jumping up and down on our beds and making a lot of noise. We must have made a lot of commotion because the lady who supervised the girl's dormitory came to see what all the rowdiness was about. She posed a question: "What is going on in here?"

Two twin girls immediately began explaining. The lady in charge curtly told them to be quiet; then, she said, "I want to hear what Rosamond has to say." I tearfully explained that we had been playing and jumping on the beds. I guess because our actions were harmless, we were not punished but were verbally corrected, and the incident was overlooked.

On another afternoon, however, I remember these same twins, along with several other girls, cornered me in the girl's dormitory. I found myself in the middle of what felt like a mini-inquisition! Looking back, I cannot remember all they said, but they were extremely critical of me. They did not like the fact that I did not have to take afternoon naps, but they had to take them. (When you are young, trivial things are big issues.) For some reason, the lady in charge of the girl's dormitory did not make me take those afternoon naps. The location for the naps was on the main floor in the large main dining room area. On that day they quizzed, criticized, and drilled me with questions and accusations. They were not happy with me at all. I should have walked away; however, when you are young, it is hard to step back and assess situations. Psychologically, a person's defense mechanism comes into play. My brother told me that he had a tough time in the boy's dormitory too. He never told me any details, but he felt my life in the girl's dormitory was a lot easier than his life in the boy's dormitory.

Everyone who lived at the orphanage referred to it as The Home. It was sponsored by the Presbyterian Church, and every Sunday, everyone went to church. This was a standard rule, no exceptions. In fact, no one would have thought of objecting to going to church. Attending Sunday school for the first time, I clearly remember my introduction to Jesus. Sitting at a small, round table, I was busily coloring Jesus' clothes in a handout sheet the Sunday school teacher had passed out to everyone. Suddenly, the boy sitting next to me looked at my picture as I was coloring it. He had an incredulous look on his face. He raised his voice and yelled, "You can't do that! You cannot color Jesus' clothes that color! His clothes are white!" Well, he set me straight about the protocol and the correct color choice concerning Jesus' attire. After his emphatic correction, I made sure I never colored Jesus' clothes any color but white.

For the main church service, adults and children all sat together. The preacher always took time to teach a short Bible lesson to the children, and then he moved on to preach his main lesson to the adults. One Sunday, one of the adults who supervised at The Home told me that my mother would be coming to the service that morning. Throughout the service, I repeatedly turned to look and check the church's side door to see if my mother had arrived. All through the service, I turned, looked, and later I turned and looked again. My mother never came to church that day.

At The Home there must have been an after-school church program for elementary students because I distinctly remember a lady talking to us about Jesus and heaven. She said there was a mansion, a house in heaven, where God prepared a place for everyone. Then, she added that all we needed to do was to ask Jesus into our hearts. So, at some point that afternoon, I remember whispering in the lady's ear that I wanted to ask Jesus into my heart. She sat me on her lap, prayed for my salvation, and spoke about that special house in heaven that God had for me.

At The Home everyone gathered at the same time each day for the dinner meal. I do not remember a breakfast or lunch routine, but I do remember the requirement for the evening meals. Everyone stood by his chair and waited for others to arrive. Then, a prayer was prayed, and we all sat down at the same time. One day, after the dinner meal, a teenager told me that I had been the topic of conversation at the head table. The reason: They were concerned because I was not eating very much. Upon hearing this report, I became scared, so after the meal, I ran upstairs to the girl's dormitory and hid under my bed. I stayed there for what seemed like a long time, but after a while, I decided it was safe to return to society. Nothing happened, and no one talked to me about my eating habits, and I was relieved.

The third Sunday of every month was set aside as visitor's Sunday for parents and relatives. Our father would come on those Sundays and bring my brother and me a bag of gum and candy. I always counted out my packages of candy and pieces of gum so they would last until the next visitor's day. One time, my brother told me he had eaten all his candy and chewed up all his gum before our father's next scheduled visit. So I sat down and counted out what I had left in my sack. I divided up my candy and gum pieces so both of us would have enough to last until our father's next visit. Our mother rarely came, but I do remember one Sunday when our father and mother both showed up on the same Sunday! What ensued was an argumentative session, which brought back memories of the constant fighting we had experienced as a family before they divorced.

Another memory I have of The Home centers on

the Christmas season. The Home always had a holiday Christmas play, which was performed for parents, relatives, visitors, and members of the Presbyterian Church. Teenagers and younger children were assigned acting parts according to the script; the lady supervisor of The Home directed the play. I remember one Christmas play; I was assigned a specific role. I do not remember the theme or storyline, but I do remember I was given the instruction at one point to walk over to another girl who was standing nearby, look her up and down, and say to her, "I'm prettier than you." Of course, everyone laughed at the audacity of a young child making such a statement. I do not know if it was this Christmas program or another one, but a family who had a daughter about my age came to see the Christmas play. Later, they called The Home and asked if they could take me on an outing for the day. I was told about the invitation and instructed to get ready because the family was picking me up for the day. When I was in the car, I mentioned that I had a brother. So, on hearing this, the husband immediately turned the car around and drove back to The Home to ask permission so my brother could join us. Well, have you ever seen the T-shirt that says, "Here comes trouble"? That was my brother! From the minute he was in the car to the time that we were dropped off, he harassed and bothered the family's young daughter. I am sure they could not wait to return us to The Home so that peace and quiet returned to their family. Needless to say, I never heard from the family again.

At The Home each child or teenager had sponsors from the Presbyterian Church; they provided Christmas gifts for everyone. I remember one Christmas season; a lady from the Presbyterian Church called and asked me what I wanted for Christmas. She said that she and two other ladies were planning to provide Christmas gifts for me; she asked me if I had a wish list. Several girls at The Home had already prompted me to have a wish list ready, so I took the wish list out of my pocket and read it over the phone. The only gift I remember requesting was a Mr. Potato Head kit. For Christmas, the ladies surprised me with two Madame Alexander dolls. You might be familiar with them; they are petite little dolls with pretty dresses. They are always "dolled up." I still have one of the dolls, but now she needs to be admitted to a doll hospital. Her head is wobbly, and some of her hair has fallen out; she is dressed in a replica of Little Riding Hood with a crocheted dress and an attached cap.

Everyone at The Home was, of course, excited about Christmas. There was a standard routine on Christmas morning. Everyone would rise early, walk single file down a flight of stairs, remain in single file formation, and head for the main dining room to eat a quick breakfast of banana and cereal. Then, we would again walk single file into another room located to the right of the dining hall. In this large room, each person had a chair with his name on it, and the gifts were all placed on this chair and on the floor next to the chair. We all scrambled to find the chair with our name on it. We all opened our gifts at the same time. I remember one particular Christmas; one of the gifts in my chair was from my mother. I was disappointed because it was a bag of hard candy. My mother may have included other items, but all I remember is the bag of hard candy.

When I was in the third grade, my father submitted papers to the court to obtain custody of my brother and me. By this time, our father had remarried. My brother and I were taken out of school to attend the court session. We were brought before a judge in his office. At that time, a family unit had to be in place before a judge would release children into parental custody. Much to my surprise, our mother was at the court for the case too.

During these judicial proceedings, the judge privately questioned my brother and me. He was concerned about our free time after school and being alone until our father and stepmother arrived home from work. Our answers must have been sufficient for the judge because he released us into our father's care before the Christmas holidays that year.

In our new family situation, meals and routines were different, of course. After one of the evening meals, I asked my father, "Do you have meals like this every night?" They had cooked a steak and made a salad, and I really do not remember what else, but I was impressed. We did not starve at The Home, but the fact that you would have steak at a meal was something new to my brother and me. Another adjustment: My brother and I had been trained at The Home to stand behind our chairs before every meal and wait for everyone to arrive. So my brother and I stood behind our chairs, waiting for everyone to come to the table. My father told us we did not need to do that anymore, so we were free to just sit down at mealtimes. During the summer of that year, we moved from Montgomery, Alabama, to Nashville, Tennessee, for a year, and the following year we moved to Gadsden, Alabama.

THE MIDDLE YEARS

Our stepmother had a daughter named Bobbie, who was about six or seven years older than my brother and me. When I was in the fourth grade, Bobbie decided she was going to start calling me "Cootie." Cootie was the name of a children's game. I did not like that name, so I decided every time she called me "Cootie," I was going to call her "Fatty." She was somewhat plump. She did not like her new name! So she complained to her mother, and then my stepmother questioned me about why I was calling Bobbie "Fatty." I told the stepmother I did not like being called "Cootie," and every time Bobbie called me "Cootie," I was going to call her "Fatty." After stating my case, the stepmother did not say anything or make a comment one way or the other about the matter. The outcome of the incident: Bobbie never called me "Cootie" again.

Within the dynamics of this blended family, there was not much peace in the home for my brother and me. The stepmother and her daughter, Bobbie, were overly critical of my brother and me, and we were blamed for many things—every day. When my brother was twelve, he decided he was going to run away from home, or I should say "bike his way" from our house to

33

our grandparent's house, which was several hundred miles away. This endeavor was to take place at night. At that time our father was working out of town and not at home. My brother did not inform me about his getaway plans. He waited until late one night to instigate his plan when he thought no one would see him. The first step in his plan began in the garage, where he geared up for his expedition. Our stepmother and Bobbie happened to see him; they just stood at the kitchen window, peering out at the garage while my brother prepared for his trip. Our stepmother told Bobbie she was going to let him leave, wait a while, and then call the police. My brother did not get far, and the police brought him back to the house. After this incident, which took place in June, my brother was then "shipped off" to Sheffield, Alabama, to our grandparent's house, which was his destination in the first place.

During that same summer, (bossy) Bobbie told me to sweep a room. She was always telling me what to do or complaining about what I did or did not do. I began sweeping, and she immediately began to criticize me. I guess because I had internalized her criticism for such a long time, something inside of me snapped. Listening to her tirade on that day could be compared to the "last straw"! When her disparagement and negative words began this time, I immediately thrust the broom toward her, and a torrent of words spewed out of my mouth! She just stood there, shocked! I would like to say this incident changed her negativism, but it did not.

Also, during those summer months, my father and stepmother divorced, and I joined my brother at our grandparent's house. Because of the divorce, my father was emotionally distraught. He talked to me about all his problems; in fact, I was placed in the role of being his counselor. Psychologically, being placed in the role of a counselor to a parent is a heavy, emotional load for a sixth grader to carry. I began having nightmares. Very late one night, for some reason, I was awakened from my sleep; I opened my eyes and saw ghosts! They were peering around the bedroom door, looking at me! This incident, along with their other nightly visits, was *very real* to me. At that time I was sleeping in a small upstairs single bedroom. My brother was upstairs too, but he was sleeping across the hall in a large bedroom that had three single beds. Our uncle, who took care of our grandparents, also slept in this large room with my brother. Because of the repeated ghostly visits, I refused to sleep by myself. So I told my brother he could sleep in the bedroom that was intended for me, and I would sleep in the large bedroom where Uncle

Bert slept because I was too scared to sleep by myself. My brother did not object to this arrangement, so we swapped bedrooms.

I thought at that time, *Surely, I would be safe with Uncle Bert's presence in the large room.* However, I saw ghosts in that room too! After several nights of these ghostly visits, I was too scared to go to sleep, so I decided I would sleep downstairs with my grandmother. Usually, the ghost appeared around 3:00 a.m., but in my grandmother's bedroom, the time element shifted; they now appeared just as dawn was breaking. When I saw the ghosts swirling above me this time, I was lying in my grandmother's bed; I started vigorously kicking the bed to distract the ghosts from coming near me. Then, as the daylight lengthened, I watched the ghosts slowly drift out the window, which was positioned next to the bed. My grandmother surmised that someone must have been talking to me. My grandfather said someone was scaring me. My grandmother did not know what to do about the situation, so she decided I needed to see a doctor and have a checkup. As a sixth grader, seeing a doctor was another mortifying experience I endured that summer. I am sure when the doctor checked my heart, he found a sixth grader who had a very rapid heartbeat. The doctor visit did not relieve my fears about going to sleep. However, the ghosts eventually left me alone, but I refused to stay in that house by myself at any time!

However, late one evening, I did find myself alone in my grandparent's house because no one had arrived home at that time. I called a school friend who lived down the street to see if I could stay at her house until someone came home. Because of my constant fear of possibly seeing the ghosts and my fear of being alone, I quickly and hurriedly walked down the sidewalk to my friend's house, half running and half walking. My friend, however, decided to hide behind some tall shrubbery bushes. These bushes were tall and perpendicular to the sidewalk, and I had to eventually pass them on my way to her house. Watching me from a distance as I hurriedly half-walked and half-ran toward her house, my friend decided to jump out in front of me as I approached the tall shrubs. Enacting her plan, she said with a great deal of volume, "Boo!" That was all it took! I screamed loudly and made a complete 360-degree spin on the sidewalk, yelling the whole time. I am sure the whole neighborhood heard me! I probably woke up a couple of snoozing dogs too.

The ghost episodes were always on my mind. One afternoon, my brother had a friend over for a

Saturday visit. They were talking and visiting on our grandparent's front porch. I told my brother's friend about the ghostly visits I was experiencing. I went into great detail about how they floated through the air and peered around the corner of the upstairs bedroom door where I was sleeping. I described the specific action of how they even followed me downstairs to my grandmother's bedroom. I must have been very descriptive, very convincing, and very emphatic about these various ghostly episodes because my brother's friend motioned to my brother by nodding his head, indicating to my brother by his body language to step over toward the front door away from me. He then spoke to my brother in a low tone and asked, "Is that really true?" I heard his question, and I yelled, "*Yes, it is!*" I am not sure I convinced him whether the ghosts were in the house or not, but I do not remember my brother's friend returning for any more visits.

Near the end of those summer months, before I entered the seventh grade, we moved to Temple, Texas, because my father had a job offer. My one thought on leaving Alabama was that I did not have to worry about those ghosts in my grandparent's house anymore. When we moved to Texas, I thought we might see cowboys and Indians like you see in the movies. However, much to my disappointment, that was not the case. At that time our family unit was three people—my father, my brother, and myself.

We lived in Temple, Texas, for one school year. At the end of that school year, we moved to Dallas, Texas. I graduated from a Dallas high school. My father was a manager of a shoe store, so he did not make a lot of money, but I was determined to go to college regardless of circumstances. Fortunately, I was awarded tuition and book scholarships each semester of my schooling. Those scholarships plus school loans provided the finances for me to attend and graduate from the University of Texas in Austin.

I met my husband, John Panzarella, at the University of Texas while he was in the process of earning his second degree. He had earned a bachelor of arts degree with a double major in math and chemistry from UT, and he continued at UT to earn a bachelor of science degree in chemical engineering. He was several years ahead of me at UT, and upon his graduation, he accepted a job with the Dow Chemical Company in Freeport, Texas. Several years later, I also graduated from UT with a bachelor of arts degree and a double major in English and history. We were married in August of that year and then settled in Lake Jackson. We have lived in Lake

Jackson, Texas, for many years; our three girls grew up in Lake Jackson. Although they have moved away, Lake Jackson is home to them. Our family's memories are in Lake Jackson, Texas.

Chapter Two

ALL THOSE AREAS WHERE
I EXPERIENCED GROWTH

STUDYING GOD'S WORD

*"And the vessel he was making from clay...he
made it over, reworking it into another vessel
as it seemed good to the potter to make it."*

Jeremiah 18:4 (AMPC)

While our three girls were growing up, we attended
St. Michael's Catholic Church. However, in 1993,
Sandra Moraw Sommerfrucht, a teacher friend, asked
me if I would like to go to church with her. I mentioned
this church invitation to John. He said, "Well, you can
go to your church, and I will go to mine." John was
being humorous, of course, but it turned out to be a
true statement because I did eventually begin attending
another church without my family.

On the following Sunday, I accompanied Sandra to
her church. While Sandra was driving me home after

church, I mentioned to her that during the service, I had seen in my mind a picture of my family. They were all standing side by side, like in a lineup, and a small flame touched the tops of their heads. The flame moved from one family member to the next and to the next, touching their heads, one after the other. As we drove along and while I was sharing this impression, Sandra immediately responded, "That is scriptural!" Later, I read in Mark 1:10 (NIV) a similar description about Jesus' baptism, where John said, "*...the Spirit descending on Him like a dove.*" That was the closest scripture reference I found at that time to relate to the impression I had seen that Sunday morning. I reflected and thought about this impression for days, and I finally concluded the Holy Spirit gave me that impression to assure me of my family's salvation.

After this initial visit, I began attending the Bible study classes at Sandra's church. The main reason for my decision was because of the Bible teacher, Mrs. Betty Bascom. She was a gifted teacher. At the first session, she proposed to everyone a goal of studying the Old and New Testament in a two-year study. She asked if that would be agreeable with everyone. The idea sounded great to all of us. For some time, I had wanted a greater understanding of the Bible.

Mrs. Bascom began, of course, with Genesis, giving background information, pointing out specific aspects of some chapters, and explaining pertinent background information and scriptures, expounding on the significance of this specific book in the Bible. This became her teaching pattern, the format to teach each book of the Bible throughout the two-year study. I would take notes, and then, during the week, I would study my notes and reread the biblical passages and scriptures Mrs. Bascom had discussed or highlighted in class. This was my study routine week after week during the two-year Bible study program.

There were times when I felt like Mrs. Bascom was speaking directly to me. I am sure others in the class felt the same way because the Holy Spirit was present in these classes. One day before the main service began, I walked over and shared with Mrs. Bascom the fact that in her class, I felt like she was speaking directly to me. As I said, I am sure everyone felt the same way about Mrs. Bascom's class because she was such an excellent teacher, but I felt that I should tell Mrs. Bascom this fact and reassure her that she was touching our hearts.

On another Sunday morning, as I was driving to church, I had an interesting experience. I just sensed that the Holy Spirit was telling me that I should tell

Pastor Charles Logan, "Thank you." This thought was so real to me that I said out loud to myself in the car, "But I never see this man before the church service!" I parked the car, walked through the front door, and entered the sanctuary. Much to my surprise, I nearly *collided* with Pastor Logan as he rounded the corner of the entryway and the sanctuary. I almost emitted a yell because I was so surprised! Words just gushed out of my mouth relating to Pastor Logan what I had just experienced in the car, and of course, I thanked him for his church and for the opportunity to study the Bible and learn God's Word.

GROWING IN BIBLICAL KNOWLEDGE

Sundays were a busy day for me; first, I attended Mrs. Bascom's Bible class, and then I rushed home and corralled my family to go to St. Michael's Church. After a few weeks of this routine, I reached a point where I decided it would just be easier to attend the Bible class and stay for the Sunday service rather than rushing here and there.

During one of these initial Sunday services, Pastor Logan walked over and quietly spoke to me. He said, "There is someone in your family you need to forgive, and when you do, the Lord's blessings will open up for you." I knew immediately who that person was; it was my father. My father was an exceedingly difficult person to live with. He could be very harsh and domineering; in fact, as my brother once said, "Dad can really be intimidating." By the time I was in high school, I had made up my mind that I was not going to marry anyone like my father. However, because of Pastor Logan's words, during my prayer time, I began talking to the Lord about my feelings, and while sitting and talking to the Lord, I forgave my father for the difficult situations, the harsh words out of his mouth, and the negative memories.

On Sunday, July 23, 1993, Pastor Logan invited a guest speaker to preach to the congregation. The evangelist preached his message and then began ministering and flowing prophetically to individuals in the congregation. He had been trained in the prophetic ministry under Dr. Hamon's Christian International Ministries in Florida. At the time I did not know anything about prophecy or the Holy Spirit speaking to a person about their life. The evangelist walked around, giving prophetic words to various individuals. When he came to me, he said, "I see you being a voice in music, singing, just singing to the Lord."

On hearing this, I said to myself, *You're not going to hear me sing!* (Singing is not one of my talents.) Then, as if the evangelist heard my thoughts, he immediately added clarification and stated, "Just between you and the Lord—that voice in music, singing... And as you begin to sing, there is just going to be a release, a freedom, and a boldness that rises up inside of you." I thought to myself, *Well, I can accept that. I can sing to myself when no one else is around.*

What happened after that was amazing! The Lord began to work in my heart, and I began to have this overwhelming desire to listen to worship music and to sing along with whoever was singing as I listened. I would listen to music in the car as I drove to and from teaching at our high school, as I ran errands, and as I worked around the house. Of course, I only sang when I was home alone because my family would have stopped, turned, and looked at me with a funny expression or perhaps even a quizzical look on their faces, wondering, I'm sure, what in the world had come over me! What was happening? The Lord was using praise and worship music to soften my hard heart and make my heart more pliable unto Him.

Time passed, and another guest speaker came to the church. This time the speaker was Pastor Stephen.

After preaching his message, Pastor Stephen walked around here and there, stopping and praying for people or giving a prophetic word. When he came to me, he stopped, placed his hand on my forehead, and said, "You will be released from a burden in your spirit." I thought to myself, *What does he mean I will be released from a burden in my spirit?* I had no idea what he was talking about! That was very puzzling to me. I kept saying to myself, *Released from a burden? What does that mean?*

Time progressed, and then a pastor from Johannesburg, South Africa, was a guest speaker at the church. After preaching, he, too, walked around, stopped, and prayed for people. I was standing next to Sandra. He prayed for Sandra, and then he came to me. He touched my forehand and said, "Oh Lord, she needs Your joy. I bind depression and discouragement in the name of Jesus and release the joy of the Lord." I said to myself, *Boy, I must really be a basket case and not even know it!*

Time passed, and then on September 1993, I received another prophetic word stating:

> "I hear the words schism or separation in your heart, and I know there has been some

type of brokenness of some kind of fellowship or relationship, and God's telling me to tell you to trust Him, trust Him. He's saying, 'Trust Me, trust Me; I'm working in ways you cannot see. Trust Me for the healing of that relationship. Trust Me, trust Me.'"

Do you know the definition of the word *schism*? I did not have a clear understanding of the definition nor how the word *schism* related to me. Sandra, my wonderful friend, wanting to help me understand my prophetic word, looked up the definition of *schism*. The dictionary defines *schism* as "a division or separation from a church or a religious body." Often, we do not immediately understand the meaning of prophetic words we receive, and in this instance, the meaning of *schism* certainly was not readily apparent to me. Sandra grasped the meaning before I did. She pointed out to me that the *schism* that had occurred in my life was my decision to stop attending St. Michael's Catholic Church with my family and my decision to attend Mrs. Bascom's Bible classes and attend the church without my family.

During a Sunday morning service, Pastor Logan gave several prophetic words to individuals, including myself. I requested a CD so that I could listen and then type the word into a written record. I had a new CD hand player, so I planned to listen as I walked a mile around my neighborhood. On this day, I had almost walked the mile, but for some reason, I did not find the exact spot on the CD that I desired, so I decided to continue walking until I located it. When I had walked about halfway down the block, I found the right spot on the CD. At that very moment, my ankles *flickered,* but it was not from any voluntary action on my part. The involuntary flickering of my ankles caused me to stumble, and I began a free fall. I was able to self-correct the fall and stop the falling motion. I thought to myself, *Good, I've got it. I will not injure my new recorder.* (Crazy things go through your mind under duress.)

However, at *that very moment*, I felt a very distinct push on my back. In fact, I was pushed with such velocity that I skidded across the sidewalk, tore a hole in my jeans, scrapped my knee very badly, and experienced a bad abrasion on my right hand. My knee throbbed so badly that I had to sit on the sidewalk for a few minutes to recover. I then slowly got up, turned, and hobbled home in the late afternoon. The next afternoon I decided to go back and find the exact spot where I had skidded to see if I had overlooked a raised section in the sidewalk or if some obstacle on the sidewalk had caused me to stumble and fall. I found the spot, but the sidewalk was flat without any raised areas or any obstructions anywhere! There was not any reason based on the evidence to explain why I fell with such velocity.

The next day at school, I was handing out papers, row by row, in one of my English classes. A few students noticed my terrible-looking scraped-up hand. They asked me what had happened. I told them that I had fallen down on the sidewalk while walking the previous evening. They laughed! Really, they were good kids, and they were a nice class, and we had a good relationship, so I looked at them and said, "You guys—you just do not have any mercy in your hearts." I knew they were not being mean; they laughed because it just seemed so strange to them that a teacher would be walking along on the sidewalk and then just fall down.

Walking was part of my daily routine, so I proceeded to walk the following day. However, this time something very unusual happened. I felt a strong impression that I was being protected. It was like I could almost see into the spiritual realm, and I had a strong inclination that four angels/soldiers were walking along with me. They were in a north, south, east, and west formation, walking very close to me. I also felt a sense of peace as I walked along. Tony Kemp, in his book *How to Partner with Angels to Usher in the Glory*, said, "*When He (the*

Holy Spirit) picks up a certain concentration of enemy forces against you, angels are released to block those forces and stop what the enemy is doing. The glory of God protects you from the enemy" Kemp 1984, 10). I can only surmise that those angels were walking along beside me to protect me. The incident was so real that I felt like I could have reached out and touched those angels; their presence was so strong.

On Friday of that same week, Sandra asked me if I would like to go with her to hear a lady pastor speak who was visiting our area. Our youngest daughter was in the band at that time and had to perform at an out-of-town football game, and John wanted to look at some tractors after work, so he would be home late; thus, I was free of any family plans. I agreed to go with Sandra.

The speaker was Pastor Marijohn, a pastor from East Texas who was gifted in the prophetic. This was the first time Sandra and I met her. The service began with praise and worship, and then Pastor Marijohn preached her message. After preaching, she began giving prophetic words to individuals. I vividly remember Pastor Marijohn speaking to a man who was still in a policeman's uniform. She looked at him and told him that he had been running from the Lord for some time, and the Lord said he would not be running anymore. I can still see this man's head in his hands at times and the pained expression on his face as he sat there, listening.

I was also one of the individuals Pastor Marijohn addressed. She looked at me and said:

> "God has given you an analytical, intellectual mind, and it's like you have to get it all in order. You have to have an understanding in here"–pointing to her head–"but in here"– pointing to her heart–"you know it's all right, but you've been trying your best to put that all together, and it's just not coming together like you would like..."

How true! All during the week, I was trying to mentally sort out and decipher all the things that had been happening to me. I was trying to bring some semblance of order into my mind. In fact, I had been in a mental quandary thinking about all that had happened. I was just perplexed about all the recent events I had experienced. Hebrews 4:13 (NIV) says, *"Nothing in all creation is hidden from God's sight. Everything is uncovered and laid bare before the eyes of him to whom we must give account."* So it should not have been a surprise to me that the Lord knew about my mental quandary. He knew that I was trying to organize things in my mind, but things were not coming together with any kind of clarification. I was just puzzled! She continued speaking prophetically to me and said:

> "God wants you to know that sometimes He just moves, and we don't really understand with our minds the things that God is doing, but He brings in the order, and He brings in His will and His direction and His way. He brings that order in our lives, and we don't always understand what's going on with our minds, but He says, 'Trust Me, trust Me,' and I feel He's been speaking that within your spirit."

So this prophetic word did not really explain *why* I was experiencing these unsettling events or *why* I was feeling confused, but at least I felt better after hearing those words.

A year or two later, Sandra and I invited Pastor Marijohn to speak in our area, and she was a guest in my home. While eating breakfast, I described to her about my walking and then falling down episode. I told her about my hurt knee, the intense pain, and my hobbling slowly home. I also informed her about the strong awareness and presence I felt of the four angels who walked along with me the next day. She commented, "There was a warring in the heavenlies." Thank goodness those four angels were protecting me and making sure I did not fall again. The Bible says in Psalm 34:7 (AMPC), *"The angel of the LORD encamps around those who fear Him [who revere and worship Him with awe] and each of them He delivers."* Those angels were my protectors, shielding me from any further harm. The Bible tells us we have angels assigned to minister, help, and protect us. Hebrews 1:14 (NIV) says, *"Are not all angels ministering spirits sent to serve those who will inherit salvation?"*

THE HOLY SPIRIT

About this time Sandra and I began attending various Christian conferences. On one occasion we went with several other ladies to a conference in Houston. After the meeting we were all in the restroom, and Sandra, standing among the ladies, mentioned that she had a headache. One of the ladies in our group immediately walked over to Sandra and said, "Let me pray for you." She proceeded to place her hand on Sandra's forehead, and she prayed for the headache to be lifted from Sandra in the name of Jesus. Suddenly, Sandra exclaimed, "It's gone! My headache is gone!" I stood there, watching and thinking to myself, *Is that really true?* I questioned in my mind whether Sandra's headache had *really* lifted off *that easily*. As you can surmise, at this point in my life, I was a "doubting Thomas."

Well, about a month later, John and I had our friends Suzie and Paul visit us from Austin, Texas. We had all been friends when we attended the University of Texas. At one point during the visit, Suzie and I were standing in our upstairs bathroom, talking. While chatting, I told Suzie I needed to go downstairs and take something for my headache. She said, "Wait a minute. Let me pray for you." She said, "Sit down." So we both sat down on the bathroom floor. Touching my forehand, she began praying for me. At that very moment, I felt a sharp, tiny sensation on the left side of my temple for just a few seconds. In those few seconds, my headache just disappeared! What had happened? The Lord was showing me, Rosamond, "the doubting Thomas," that healing was real, and yes, I was certainly convinced by this experience that Sandra had really been healed of her headache! It is nothing to the Lord to underscore a point by repeating a healing, right? Plus, when you think about it, the Lord even repeated the same location—a bathroom! Both headache experiences had taken place in a bathroom setting, and Sandra and I were relieved of our headaches. All I can say is the Lord has a sense of humor, underscoring the fact that He is in the "healing business"—even today.

During this time Sandra lent me a book titled *The*

Holy Spirit and You by Dennis and Rita Bennett. I read the book, and I especially focused on Chapter 5, which discussed baptism in the Holy Spirit. At the beginning of Chapter 5, the authors ask the reader the question, "Who is going to baptize you in the Holy Spirit?" They answered their own question, stating, "Jesus is going to do it!" (Bennett 1971, 56). The authors proceeded to instruct the reader on how to receive this baptism in the Holy Spirit and thus one's prayer language. I decided the only place to read in complete privacy, where I would not be interrupted and where I could concentrate as I contemplated Chapter 5, was sequestered in the bathroom. I am sure moms can relate to this need to "sequester" sometimes from the family. So I took the book, opened it to Chapter 5, read it again and again, and focused on following the instructions on how to receive baptism in the Holy Spirit. While following the instructions, I received the ability to speak in the language of the Holy Spirit in the blink of an eye. I just followed the instructions in the book, and the Holy Spirit showed up!

One day after school, Sandra asked me if I would go with her to visit a pastor in Freeport who moved in the prophetic. At that time, Sandra was seeking spiritual direction concerning some family issues. However, she did not know the church's phone number, so she called several friends and was given the number. She called the church and made an appointment to speak with the pastor, Pastor Janette. When we arrived at the church, Pastor Janette was busy and mentioned that perhaps we should come back at another time. However, Sandra is a communicator, and she just kept conversing and talking with her. Then, suddenly, the pastor began giving Sandra prophetic words and instructions that related to her family situation.

Then, the pastor turned to me. She said that the Lord was showing her a vision of a tree that had many cocoons on it. There was a large snake in the tree that was feasting on the Christians who needed deliverance from these cocoons. In the spirit realm, Pastor Janette saw herself shaking the tree, and people started falling out of these cocoons and running joyously around. Pastor Janette then turned to me and said the Lord was healing me of some deep wounds and abuses that I had suffered; she also said chains were falling off, and I was coming out of a cocoon.

As we were leaving, I turned and said to Pastor Janette, "At some time or other, I would like to speak to your congregation and tell them what the Lord has done in my life." My intentions were to share what the Lord had recently done in my life. I had no intention of sharing anything about my family or about past experiences. The pastor did not say *yes* or *no*, but I went home and began typing up my notes. When my notes were complete, I stopped and said to myself, *Wait a minute, the Lord has not told me to do anything with these notes*. I said to myself, *I will just set my notes aside and wait*.

On July 17, 1996, Sandra and I visited Pastor Janette's church for a Sunday evening service. While speaking to the congregation, Pastor Janette turned to me and said, "Get ready to give your testimony. You have held it on file long enough. Start speaking your testimony." Pastor Janette had no idea that I had even been working on my testimony.

At another Sunday evening service, Sandra and I again attended Pastor Janette's Sunday evening service. At one point while speaking, Pastor Janette stopped, looked at me, and said, "The Lord says it is time." That was all she said to me. Taking that as a cue, I talked with her after the service about my notes. She agreed with me about sharing them at her church, so I worked on them some more. Then, I called Pastor Janette and told her I was ready to give my testimony. We agreed on a Sunday evening date.

SHARING WITH OTHERS

The Sunday evening date arrived for me to speak at Pastor Janette's church. Sitting there and waiting to speak, I continually prayed for the Lord to give me strength. Then, the time came for me to share. Pastor Janette called me forth. She said, "Come, Rosamond, come, and let God pray with you for strength." As we all know, God is omniscient. Just a few seconds before, I was sitting and praying and silently asking the Lord to give me strength to speak. Now, verbally, via this pastor, God was reassuring me that He would give me the strength to speak and to share with others what He wanted me to share.

I walked and mounted the step-up area to the podium. I stood there silently for a minute. I could not speak! My jaws were locked! Opening your mouth to speak is an everyday occurrence, but I literally could not physically open my mouth! It was not from stage fright or anything like that! I had a challenging time just trying to pry open my mouth for those words to come out. This seems like such a simple thing—to just open your mouth and speak, but my jaws were locked! I stood there silently for another moment. Then, through tightly clenched teeth, I spoke to the audience and shared that I had been praying for the Lord to give me strength. Immediately, when I spoke those words, Pastor Janette, who was sitting on the front row, said loudly, "Amen!" In the spiritual realm, something happened! Instantly, my jaws unlocked! It was as if a lever had been released in the heavenly realm, and my jaws opened! Just like that! I actually felt a physical release, and the muscles in my jaws relaxed; then, I was able to open my mouth and speak! Think of that—the pastor of the church just said one simple word, *amen*, but this was the spiritual key that released my locked jaws so I could speak freely to the people.

I shared with the congregation that I always listened to Dr. Dobson's radio program as part of my morning routine while getting ready for school. I also shared with the congregation that in the previous week, Dr. Dobson had interviewed a young girl who had experienced a tremendous trauma in her home life. She related to Dr. Dobson's radio audience that her stepfather had placed a gun to her temple and said, "I'm going to kill you!" She was very calm retelling this horrific incident. There were no tears. There was not any anxiousness or anxiety in her voice nor any fear. She calmly related her story to the radio audience. I kept telling myself that if that young girl could go on a national radio program and calmly and methodically tell her dramatic story and discuss the dire and frightening situation she had experienced, then I should be able to come to a church, open my mouth, and share what I knew the Lord wanted me to share.

I told the listening audience that I do not go around freely talking or sharing about my childhood. In fact, I had closed that *door* and had deliberately locked that *door*. I do remember telling the congregation that while I was praying about speaking to them, I received a strong impression. I saw a door that had three locks on it; one lock was near the top of the door, the second lock was a little distance down from the first lock, and the third lock was below the second lock. I knew those locks represented moments in my life where I had locked away the things I had experienced, and I did not really care to share or discuss them.

However, I also realized that the locks on those three doors symbolized just how much I was willing to share with someone about my past. Sometimes if I felt I could trust someone, I would unlock one lock, revealing something or an incident from my childhood or just generally my past. At another time I would unlock two locks if I felt that I could really trust that person, but rarely did I ever unlock all three locks and share with anyone. I had locked those memories away, and I really did not want to think about them anymore. However, that Sunday evening, I knew the Lord wanted me to unlock all three locks and share with everyone. I told the church members my original intention was to share with them what the Lord had done in my life over the last five years, but I added that I knew that was not the Lord's purpose for me. He wanted me to openly share all three locks on all three doors.

I told those listening that I understood more clearly the Lord's plan on instructing Abraham to take his son Isaac to Mount Moriah. The Lord was testing Abraham, and Abraham obeyed. So, now, I was being tested. Would I obey? We can all look back, I am sure, and reflect on how the Lord checks our sincerity and our obedience to Him as we continue in our spiritual walk.

With this audience I shared my early childhood, my middle school years, and my high school years. I shared that my mother left my brother and me alone all the time and many, many nights. We were two young children who were often scared. There were a few times at night when our father would come and stay with us, but by nine o'clock, he had to leave so he could get some sleep and be ready for work the next day. I also shared with them the fact that my father was very intimidating and verbally abusive at times, and over the years I developed a hard heart toward him because of his harsh words and actions.

Later, when my father was elderly, my brother tried to find a nursing home for him near the Fort Worth area where he lives, but he was not successful, so he called me and asked if I would try to find a nursing home in my area. I could not teach school and take care of my father's physical needs as he aged. Fortunately, I did find an opening at a nursing home in Angleton, Texas, so I began the routine of visiting my father several times during the week at the end of a school day.

When I finished speaking, the pastor told me she was glad to hear that I had found a place for my father, and I had forgiven him and had taken care of him.

A BREAKTHROUGH

In May 1994, at a Sunday evening service, Pastor Logan was preaching, and toward the end of his message, he asked everyone to come toward the front. As he was speaking, I was standing some distance from him, but at one point, he paused and looked my way. He was looking directly at me, his eyes "locked" with my eyes, and at that very moment, something dropped into my chest. I was standing next to my friend Sandra, and when that happened, I said to her, "I felt that!" I felt something transcend from the spirit realm into the physical realm and drop into my chest! Still looking at me, Pastor Logan immediately said, "I need to get over there!" By the time he came to me, I felt such a heavy weight on my shoulders that I just wanted to sit down; I felt like I just could not physically stand up. Pastor Logan came and stood in front of me, and all I could say to him was, "Just let me go; I don't think I can stand up much longer." He replied, "You must stand and listen to what I have to tell you." Then, he proceeded to tell me, "The Lord says He is going to honor you because of your reverential fear of Him." He continued, saying, "There has been a narrowness of understanding of who Jesus is, and the Lord is going to open up that narrowness of understanding."

When Pastor Logan finished speaking to me, I immediately started coughing. My coughing sounded like someone who had a bad case of pneumonia with a lot of lung congestion. When I finally did stop coughing, Pastor Logan said, "Don't anyone touch her! She has had a breakthrough." After the service I talked with Pastor Logan about what had happened, and he told me that in the spiritual realm, he had seen heaven open up above my head when he had looked my way. Scripture lays the groundwork for a spiritual breakthrough in Ezekiel 36:25 (AMPC), which says, "*Then will I sprinkle clean water upon you, and you shall be clean from all your uncleanness...*" The Holy Spirit had been working in my heart and "cleaning me up." And Ezekiel 36:26 (AMPC) follows with, "*A new heart will I give you, and a new spirit will I put within you, and I will take away the stony heart out of your flesh and give you a heart of flesh.*" That was what happened to me. The Lord was giving me a new heart. He took away my stony, hard heart.

However, I am sure before this breakthrough, the Lord, in His mercy, looked at my heart and said, "This is a really hard heart; it's going to take some daily work on My part to create a soft and pliable heart—a new heart for this lady." You might ask yourself, *How did the Lord go about transforming her heart?* The Holy Spirit used my daily routine of reading the Word, studying the Word, listening to praise and worship music, and singing (when no one was around) to transform my heart.

SPIRIT-ANOINTED PRAYERS

Besides my daily Bible reading, I also read a lot of Christian books. One book, *The Believer's Authority* by Kenneth Hagin, made an impression on me. In Chapter 1, Hagin wrote, "*The authority of the believer is unveiled more fully in the Book of Ephesians than any other epistle written to the churches*," and he also informed the reader that "*...there are Spirit-anointed prayers at the end of the first and third chapters*" (Hagin 1985, 1). Following are the two scriptures Hagin highlighted.

> *I have not stopped giving thanks for you, remembering you in my prayers. I keep asking that the God of our Lord Jesus Christ, the glorious Father, may give you the Spirit of wisdom and revelation, so that you may know him better. I pray that the eyes of your heart may be enlightened in order that you may know the hope to which he has called you, the riches of his glorious inheritance in his holy people, and his incomparably great power for us who believe. That power is the same as the mighty strength he exerted when he raised Christ from the dead and seated him at his right hand in the heavenly realms.*

Ephesians 1:16-20 (NIV)

For this reason I kneel before the Father, from whom every family in heaven and on earth derives its name. I pray that out of his glorious riches he may strengthen you with power through his Spirit in your inner being, so that Christ may dwell in your hearts through faith. And I pray that you, being rooted and established in love, may have power, together with all the Lord's holy people, to grasp how wide and long and high and deep is the love of Christ, and to know this love that surpasses knowledge—that you may be filled to the measure of all the fullness of God.

Ephesians 3:14-19 (NIV)

What impressed me about Hagin's book is that he said that he read those scriptures over and over and prayed over them out loud two or three times a day for six months! Hagin also said we need the spirit of wisdom and revelation of Christ and His Word if we are to grow spiritually. So, upon reading Hagin's commentary, I decided to add these two scriptures to my daily prayer time. I have prayed these two Ephesian scriptures daily for years so that I may continue to grow in the wisdom and revelation knowledge of God.

GOD'S PLAN

As I stated in the preface, the Lord has numerous ways to instruct us and order our steps. However, for me, the greatest influence and direction in my life have been prophetic words. Some prophetic words have been spoken to me at Christian conferences, others sent via mail or emailed, and others have been spoken by pastors in church settings. Dr. Hamon, founder of Christian International Ministries International (CIMI), wrote a book titled *Prophets and Personal Prophecy*. In his book Dr. Hamon stated that personal prophecy is God's revelation of His purpose for a person, a family, or a group of people. He explained the importance of prophecy and stated in his book that "*When God speaks something, it is decreed in heaven. It is impregnated into the spirit of the person receiving the word of the Lord, and God's word carries with it the creative, life-giving power of self-fulfillment*" (Hamon 1993, 64).

So prophetic words, whether spoken to an individual, a family, or a group of people, are God's divine directive and purpose for them. Over the years prophetic words have often been spoken to me at just the right time. They have certainly encouraged and comforted me many, many times, and I have often received prophetic words at the very moment I needed that comfort or edification.

Dr. Hamon also said in his book that when someone receives a prophetic word, he should type it out and pray over it. Through the years I have followed that practice. By praying over a prophetic word, revelation and clarity to its meaning are often revealed by the Holy Spirit. On the other hand, sometimes prophetic words are about the future, and usually we will not understand the meaning until we have experienced that situation. There are times when it takes years to understand a prophetic word and really grasp its meaning and the Lord's purpose. Reflecting on prophetic words I have received, I am now able to see how the Lord has "steered me" in the direction He wanted me to go. What did not make sense at the time now makes sense after the passage of time. A pastor once said to me, "You do not understand the depth of a prophetic word until you walk it out." After looking over my prophetic words as I planned this book, I am now able to understand more clearly how God's prophetic direction "steered" me to fulfill the purposes and plans He wanted me to accomplish. For example, the following words are much clearer to me now than at the time they were spoken. At the time, I had no clue what they meant.

On September 13, 1994, there was a guest speaker at Pastor Logan's church. The guest speaker preached his message and then spoke prophetic words to several individuals. Then, in a prophetic utterance to those in attendance, he said:

> "The word I just got in my spirit is education. I don't know whether you're a teacher in the church, but I don't believe you are. You have something to do with the school system or something to do with the people that are involved in the education system, and the Lord is going to use you in a greater way. If you're that person, then come up here right now, and I'm going to pray for you... Has something to do with education. You have the ability to influence people that are in that arena. Amen."

Sandra Moraw Sommerfrucht, my teacher friend, stepped forward. Since the implication of this word seemed to imply one person, I hesitated and did not step forward. Then, the Holy Spirit brought further clarification because the speaker immediately followed with the words, "I feel the word...*rose*...in my spirit. Does anyone have the name Rose?"

Well, I was the only person in attendance with the word *rose* in their name, so I stepped forward. What was the Lord doing? The Lord was letting me know that I, along with Sandra, was called in the educational realm to carry out His plan, whatever it was. Neither of us had a clue what those prophetic words meant. Isn't that intriguing how the Lord used a prophetic word to let me know that I, too, was to participate in His plan when I was not even sure that I should step forward and join Sandra? The Lord had a future endeavor for Sandra and me to carry out.

Sandra and I, of course, had no idea what the prophetic words "in the greater way" meant. We were not given any specific instructions; we were just given a general prophetic word about *education*. In Dr. Hamon's book on prophecy that I have mentioned, he stated that unless you are given specific instructions in a prophetic word, you are to continue to do what you are doing and trust the Lord.

Four months later, in January 1994, Pastor Marijohn, whom I have mentioned before, prophesied more details about God's purpose in a word to Sandra and me in Dallas/Garland, Texas. She said to us:

> "I'm calling you to stand on your feet and to gird yourself for the race that is ahead of thee. Prepare yourself now; for yea, there is a race that is just before thee... You shall run it for

Me, and you shall run it not hindered by the weights and confines and the restrictions of this world, but you shall run it for Me..."

Hebrews 12:1 (AMPC) speaks about the race believers run and says:

...let us strip off and throw aside every encumbrance (unnecessary weight) and that sin which so readily (deftly and cleverly) clings to and entangles us, and let us run with patient endurance and steady and active persistence the appointed course of the race that is set before us.

So Sandra and I received some words about *education* and *running a race.* That was all the prophetic direction we were given; there were not any specific instructions about how, where, or when. Nothing!

A year and a half later, on May 30, 1995, Sandra and I drove to the Dallas/Garland area to hear Pastor Marijohn preach; this began our yearly visits to hear Pastor Marijohn preach and to listen to her as she moved prophetically in individuals' lives and spoke words to those in attendance.

At this meeting Pastor Marijohn prophesied again to Sandra and me about *a race* and the *educational area,* but the Holy Spirit added the following words, stating, "The Lord says you are going to stand against humanism in a brand-new way...and truths of the gospel you're going to declare." As I have said, we did not have any understanding of what the words meant or where these prophetic words would eventually lead us.

Four months later, in September 1995, Dr. Hamon's ministry, Christian International Ministries, sent me a prophetic word via a CD. This word alluded to the future and added more details stating that I would be "looking and digging into books." This ministry person also said to me, "I feel a real strong teaching anointing upon your life, and I see you looking into books and looking into dictionaries and just digging and digging."

So, at this point, I understood that I would be "standing against humanism in a brand-new way," and I would be "digging into reading material and various books," but I did not have any clue as to what all this meant. So I continued my normal daily routine. Other than that, no other specific instructions were given in that word. Because of this word, Sandra did, however, give me for my birthday an in-depth book about the priesthood in the Old Testament.

Three years later, in June 1998, Pastor Marijohn held her regular monthly meeting in Garland, Texas, and Sandra and I traveled to Garland to hear her preach, teach, and give prophetic words. At that time Pastor Marijohn prophesied to Sandra and me that "There is a new assignment...new things that I am calling you to do... There are some new steps ahead of each of you... new things that He's calling you to participate in and enter in and to move with Him in these new things."

In retrospect these words are so much clearer to me now because I have experienced them. At the time, of course, I kept wondering, *What is this new assignment?* and *What are the new things?* and *What am I supposed to be doing?* However, this is how the Lord works. We are to walk by faith. If we understood every prophetic word we received, we would not be walking by faith, right?

Two months later, in August 1998, Sandra and I received some additional prophetic words about education. This prophetic word spoke about "...a new uncharted course...ministry of a platform in a strange and unusual way."

Again, there were not any specific instructions. At that time these prophetic words were just pieces to a puzzle. The Lord was giving us a little piece here and a little piece there. Now, in retrospect, I see how all the puzzle pieces fit together.

All during this time, however, the Lord continued working in my heart, clearing out the debris from the hurts and all the wounds I experienced while growing up. Several years later, during a Wednesday evening service, I was thinking to myself, *Why am I not asked to do more for the Lord?* Remember the Lord is omniscient. A few minutes later, Pastor Logan motioned for me to step over to him. He quietly said to me, "I see a question mark over your head. The Lord wants you to know there are some things He is working on."

Isn't that remarkable? I had a question in *my mind*, and the Lord answered it immediately! At that time I reminded myself of Hebrews 4:13 (NIV), which says, *"Nothing in all creation is hidden from God's sight."* The Lord answered my very question! I was just standing there, thinking those thoughts, and the Lord used Pastor Logan to answer my question—at that very moment! The Lord was letting me know He needed to work on some more things in my heart. Evidently, He had "a lot of cleaning up to do."

AN UNCHARTED COURSE

In the spring of 1999, a bulletin was sent out to Brazosport Independent School (BISD) teachers, asking them to submit any new proposals they might have for a course; the proposals were to be submitted to the school board for committee evaluation. Seizing the moment, my teacher friend Sandra wrote and submitted a proposal for a Bible course to be offered at Brazoswood High School as an elective. Numerous school districts in Texas were already teaching as an elective a Bible course in their schools, so precedence had been set in our favor. The BISD course committee read and studied Sandra's proposal and then presented it to the school board for a vote. After some discussion and deliberation, the school board approved the Bible course. We were given the green light to teach this new Bible course as an elective for the 1999–2000 school year. Our prophetic words were materializing before our eyes, and at the time, we did not even realize it!

The Facts, our local newspaper, wrote an article about the new elective course and BISD's board approval; they placed it on the front page! *The Facts'* article was titled "Bible Class Gets Blessing of BISD Trustees." In the article BISD's director of instruction stated, "The course will be historical in nature. We studied other school districts that are teaching it, and they had no problems." This was an uncharted course for our school district, and this was the unchartered course that had been mentioned in our prophetic word.

People are always surprised to learn that teaching a Bible course as an elective in public schools in Texas is legal. Other states also offer similar Bible courses. The Supreme Court clarified the issue of teaching the Bible in public schools and set the perimeters stating that teaching of religion in public schools must be objective and academic, not devotional. The course's purpose was to teach students biblical history, study aspects of how the Bible was developed, and present an understanding of the Bible's influence on people and our culture.

The course's title was Bible History and Literature, and the course was based on the National Council on Bible Curriculum in Public Schools' curriculum. Sandra ordered their curriculum, which provided a teaching outline for the Old and New Testaments. In their Bible curriculum, they provided some sample classroom activities and sample model lessons for us to study and incorporate into our lesson plans.

In Sandra's proposal to the school board, she pointed out that the Bible has always had a historical influence on America. Her proposal highlighted the importance of the Bible and its impact on American culture and literature, and thus, she stated in her proposal that because of this fact, the Bible should be studied. One argument expressed by Sandra was the fact that there are many biblical references in American short stories, novels, and plays that students read and study as they progress through school, especially in high school English courses. Another point Sandra made in her proposal was that students should study the Bible in order to have a greater understanding of biblical symbols, analogies, implications, and references as they read various types of literature.

In sophomore English, which I taught, Shakespeare's *Julius Caesar* has many biblical references, and I always pointed them out to students. For example, in 2 Samuel 31, King Saul was wounded in battle at Mount Gilboa, and he asked his armor-bearer to thrust a sword through his body to quicken his death. He did not want the Philistines to capture him and parade him through the streets in shame, which was a custom after a battle in that era. King Saul's armor-bearer refused to obey King Saul's command, so King Saul chose to die by thrusting himself onto his own sword. Then, King Saul's armor-bearer, seeing his leader die, chose to fall on his own sword and die too.

Shakespeare wrote a similar battle scene in *Julius Caesar*. Shakespeare had Brutus, one of the battle commanders, experience a similar death scene. Brutus and Cassius were losing the battle. Brutus told his armor-bearer to thrust his sword into him. Like King Saul's armor-bearer, Brutus' armor-bearer refused the command. Brutus then fell on his own sword, and his armor-bearer, following his commander's lead, also killed himself by falling on his own sword.

When I taught *Julius Caesar*, I would always read the biblical battle scene in 2 Samuel 31 *before* reading Shakespeare's portrayal of a similar battle in *Julius Caesar*. There were other biblical references in this play, and I always stopped and pointed them out to the students. I told the students that if they did not catch these biblical references interwoven in the play, they would miss many innuendos as they read. The fact is that students who read and study the Bible have a greater understanding and insight into the literature they study.

This elective Bible course was categorized as history in the curriculum and classified under the auspices of the history department. However, all budget requests for supplies and teaching material for the upcoming school year had already been submitted by a March deadline, and March was the month the school board had approved the new Bible course. So Sandra and I had a problem. We did not have an opportunity to submit a budget request for classroom supplies to the history department. However, we did have a list of needs: a classroom set of Bibles, Bible dictionaries, concordances, maps, plus DVDs, and other related books and supplies.

What did we do? We asked our principal for permission to appeal to local churches for donations for this new course. Then, Sandra and I made appointments and met with several pastors in our area, sharing with them about this new Bible course. Several churches were generous in their giving. One small church gave $1,000! A larger church gave $500; however, we also received small donations from various churches. With this money we began the 1999 school year with a classroom set of twenty-five Bibles, fifteen Bible dictionaries, fifteen concordances, and fifteen biblical reference maps. We even had enough money to purchase much-needed movies, CDs, and other visual supplies. The CDs and other visual material were extremely helpful because visualization really helped students to connect biblical characters' names to their roles in the Bible.

OPPOSITION

However, I must add that not everything went smoothly. One individual in the community called our principal and complained about us asking churches for donations for the Bible course. Then, I received a call from our principal. Sandra was out of town at the time. The principal told me not to request any more money from any church; however, the money we had gathered by that time was sufficient to purchase our supplies to begin the school year.

A SACK OF MONEY

At one of Pastor Marijohn's Dallas/Garland meetings, she, at the end of a meeting, made the announcement that anyone who did not receive a prophetic word but still desired one to form a prayer line. She then prayed for each person. Sandra joined the line of people. As she was praying for Sandra, Pastor Marijohn told Sandra that she saw in the spirit realm a sack of money. Later, Sandra mentioned that the sack of money that Pastor Marijohn referenced could have been the money that was generously donated by area churches for the new Bible course.

THE BUSY, BUSY SUMMER

During those summer months, Sandra and I were very busy preparing for the Bible classes. We began writing and generating innumerable class lessons. We created student activities for various lessons. We devised art assignments for scriptural studies, typed questions for Bible passage readings, listened to and previewed CDs, and composed tests for the upcoming 1999–2000 school year. We planned out the division of labor for books in the Old and New Testaments. For instance, we took Genesis and decided on a logical division of Genesis between the two of us. We also previewed biblical movies and typed lessons to guide students as they watched these movies.

Sandra created assignments and lessons for the first half of Genesis; I created assignments and lessons for the second half of Genesis. When we finished our work, we combined and compiled the work together into a Genesis unit. We followed this same process for creating and compiling lessons in the Old and New Testament for the Bible curriculum.

We wrote letters and asked permission from numerous authors and publishers for their approval to use their published material. For example, we received permission from the author of a Bible coloring book to use her illustrations. This artist had drawn pictures depicting aspects of biblical characters and numerous Bible stories. For one of the art assignments, Sandra used this author's depiction of creation for a Genesis project; pictures were used from the coloring book. Students followed instructions for a unique art assignment based on the seven days of creation. According to day one, two, three, etc., of creation, students were to sequence in the correct order the days of creation, add a Scripture verse for each picture, and then add their own captions describing what took place on each day. Students were given art assignments for the ark of the covenant and the Ten Commandments. There were many other art assignments the students created during the school year. Hopefully, the student's self-esteem was enhanced by seeing their completed artwork on display in the classroom on the bulletin board.

In a New Testament assignment, several map lessons were created and assigned. For example, one map lesson was assigned to help students clarify locations and places where Jesus walked and performed miracles. For other instructions students were assigned lessons on Proverbs. For example, students were instructed to illustrate in art form Proverbs 4:11–12, 20–23. Students' artwork was impressive for this assignment and other New Testament art assignments.

Writing a curriculum for a complete school year was too big of a project for one person. Ecclesiastes 4:9 (NIV) says, *"Two are better than one because they have a good return for their labor."* With the two of us working together, we did have a good return on our labor; we accomplished tasks and created a Bible curriculum for the Old and New Testament for the upcoming school year by the end of summer. That summer, we were very busy; our computers and our hands had little rest.

THE UMBRELLA

Another prophetic word Sandra and I received referred to an analogy about an umbrella. The prophetic word stated, "It would be like an umbrella; we would see it." When those words were spoken to us, we did not understand what the "it" meant; however, as we worked that summer, the curriculum expanded, and it did indeed open up like an umbrella. Only in retrospection and as time passed did the understanding of the word *umbrella* become apparent. Like the apostles who did not readily grasp the impact of Jesus' teachings or His resurrection power when it occurred, Sandra and I did not readily grasp the meaning of those prophetic words until later. We could be compared to Peter in our thinking. After Jesus rose from the dead, Peter's initial reaction was to say to the other disciples, "I'm going fishing." Neither Peter nor the other disciples understood what had really happened, and neither Sandra nor I fully understood our prophetic words at that time. It is often difficult to understand the Lord's purpose for our lives as we are "walking through the events."

One thing is for sure: Even though you may create and write a curriculum, you begin to really learn the material as you teach it. I found the Bible-based videos and movies helpful in learning biblical genealogy and the characters' names. These historical movies helped me to visualize in my mind Jacob and Esau and other characters in the Bible. I learned a lot, and hopefully, my students did too.

THE CLASSROOM

Most of my students who chose to take the elective course attended a church, but I was really surprised at what they did not know. For instance, we analyzed and discussed many proverbs. I particularly remember one class discussion concerning Proverbs 25:11 (AMPC), which says, "*A word fitly spoken and in due season is like apples of gold in settings of silver.*" I was surprised at the student's lack of understanding of this proverb, so hoping to help them, I then said, "This word is aptly spoken."

I thought the meaning would be obvious to the students, but they still did not readily grasp its implications. In fact, we spent extended class time discussing its meaning. Students would offer suggestions as to what they thought Proverb 25:11 meant, but they would miss the mark, so to speak. Then, another student would offer a different explanation or add an additional comment to what had just been spoken. I kept repeating over and over; this word is "*fitly or aptly spoken.*" After some lengthy discussion, one student finally grasped the idea and said, "A word fitly spoken is a word spoken at exactly the right moment; it is spoken at the exact moment when it is needed for the hearer to hear those words."

In another class session, we studied questions about Exodus. In Exodus 32:26, Moses became angry with the Israelites because they created the golden calf while he was on the mountain with God for forty days. Returning to the camp, Moses stood before the people and angrily asserted to them, "...*Whoever is on the Lord's side, let him come to me. And all the Levites [the priestly tribe] gathered together to him*" (Exodus 32:26, AMPC). In our discussion, I drew an imaginary line with my hand and told the class that, essentially, Moses had drawn an "imaginary line in the sand." This line was for those who chose to immediately stand with him; essentially, whoever stepped over this imaginary drawn line joined Moses against their rebellion. The Levites were the *first* group to step over this imaginary line and join Moses. Because of this act, the Levites were redeemed, according to Scripture, from their earlier revenge, deceit, and treatment of Hamor and his son, Shechem, concerning the treatment of their sister, Dinah. The Levites' redemption occurred because they chose to support Moses. While discussing this event with the class, I sensed in class in the spiritual realm a "big, silent thud"! The students just sat there, looking at me wide-eyed! I could almost see question marks in their eyes.

After class, I kept pondering that moment and those question marks that I had seen in their eyes; it finally occurred to me. The class lacked any background understanding about the Levites. They were not able to make the connection that the Levites were redeemed from their heinous crime and behavior because of their obedience to Moses' command. The next day, I reread to them Exodus 32:29 (AMPC), which states, "*And Moses said [to the Levites, by your obedience to God's command] you have consecrated yourselves today [as priests] to the Lord...that the Lord may restore and bestow His blessing upon you this day.*" I discussed this passage and reviewed the temple duties of the Levites versus a priest's duties and responsibilities. Hopefully, they understood more clearly about obedience to the Lord, the Levites' decision and their stand, and the temple duties of the Levitical priest.

Each year, Sandra and I added new activities and supplemental readings to the Bible course for added interest and variety of activities. We even decided to study the book of Revelation during the last six weeks of school because students knew very little about Revelation and most likely had never studied Revelation chapter by chapter.

Sandra and I taught these Bible classes for three years. Then, in the fourth year, there was a statewide monetary crunch that affected all school districts in Texas. BISD was forced to scale back on numerous classes, and at the same time, there was a growing emphasis on the state-mandated STAR tests. At first these tests were designated just for tenth-grade English classes; however, eventually, other core subjects were added. Because of these changes, I was reassigned to teach all English classes and no Bible classes. Sandra taught her English classes but was able to continue teaching one Bible class each year until she retired.

TWO ADDITIONAL CURRICULUMS

Sandra and I proceeded to write another curriculum that emphasized godly character in students' lives. The curriculum's focus was based on the nine fruits of the Spirit—love, joy, peace, patience, kindness, goodness, faithfulness, and self-control—discussed in Galatians 5:22–23. Because I spent so much time working on this curriculum, my husband commented that I must be writing a *War and Peace* novel. By this time, Sandra and her husband had moved to the Dallas area. So, in the Houston area, I promoted this curriculum by contacting numerous churches and private Christian schools, but nothing materialized from these visits. I spoke to school supervisors, met with principals, and had one-on-one meetings with teachers, but nothing of substance came out of these meetings. Evidently, that educational avenue was not the Lord's plan for this curriculum.

At that time we thought the character curriculum was the one the Lord planned to use in a "*greater way*," but in retrospect, the Lord's purpose and "the greater way" was the Bible curriculum we had taught at the high school.

Sandra and I also co-authored another Christian-based curriculum for the purpose of teaching manners and etiquette to students based on Scripture and biblical stories, accompanied with various activities. We taught this curriculum in Mansfield, which is an area south of Dallas. However, nothing of significance materialized from this curriculum either. Proverbs 19:21 (AMPC) says, "*Many plans are in a man's mind, but it is the Lord's purpose for him that will stand.*" Although we spent a great deal of time developing these two curriculums, they evidently were not the Lord's plan because doors did not readily open to implement either curriculum.

Chapter Three

ALL THOSE AREAS
WHERE I WALKED
THROUGH THE FLAMES

THE SHOCK WAVES

"...you may be distressed by trials and suffer temptations, so that [the genuineness] of your faith may be tested..."

First Peter 1:6-7 (AMPC)

In today's chaotic world, it is an accepted fact that individuals or family members will most likely experience job loss at some point in their career. Today, if a company decides, for whatever reason, to downsize, lay a person off, or just let an employee go, these actions do not create a stir or much of a response from anyone; they are just an accepted way of life in society today. No one is surprised to hear about a friend, an acquaintance, or a family member who loses his job for whatever reason. Nowadays, people have even lost their jobs if they did not have a COVID vaccine shot, and, of course, because of COVID, jobs were curtailed, people experienced unemployment, and others had sharply curtailed working hours.

Likewise, in the 1990s and early 2000, the job market began shifting. Companies began releasing individuals from their jobs because of various reasons— downsizing, lacking company profit, or rearranging personnel. During this time, our family experienced these shifting patterns in the job market. After graduating from college and working for six months, two of our three daughters were laid off from their jobs. Needlessly to say, it was a devastating experience for them; just out of college, they entered the job market, and six months later, they no longer had a job.

On the other hand, our oldest daughter, after being employed by an established insurance company for fifteen years, was also laid off from her job. She, along with several other employees, was let go because the company's profits were down, and the company's payroll needed to be reduced. I am sure everyone can share similar stories during this tumultuous time. The reality was that most anyone could be laid off from their job. At that time one headline in *The Houston Chronicle* stated, "Halliburton cuts 650 jobs in western states." Nowadays, no one reacts to such headlines or news reports.

In what now seems like centuries ago, there was a time in the workforce when employees expected to work for a company for thirty years and retire with their 401(k) along with their company's retirement plan. Working for a company for thirty years was the mindset of most employees in 1993. This was also the expectation of many Dow Chemical employees at that time. Salaried employees just assumed that "Daddy Dow" would give them a thirty-year pin, and then they would retire and enjoy their retirement years. However, 1993 was the year that Dow Chemical made changes in its business model. Dow Chemical decided to not only cut hourly employees, who were usually the first group of employees to be laid off, but the company also made the decision to lay off salaried employees. This was a change in Dow's business practice. The very first salaried employees to be affected by this new Dow policy were my husband, a chemical engineer, and a friend, who was also a chemical engineer. Dow's decision sent shock waves through the community. In fact, at the time, the local newspaper, *The Facts*, had daily headlines and lengthy articles about Dow Chemical and the company's actions and new decisions.

As I stated, this time period in the business world seems like centuries ago.

The Lord was gracious to our family and eased the initial shock of a pending layoff because John learned of his planned dismissal from Dow Chemical about two months prior to the actual occurrence. Fortunately, John had a boss who liked him. One late Sunday afternoon, John's boss called and asked if he could come over and talk to John. I did not think too much about his request because John's boss was to be married in a month or two, so I just assumed he was seeking some marital insights from John. Upon his arrival, John and the boss went to our patio and stayed a long time. I was busy with the girls, finishing supper dishes, checking their schoolwork assignments, and getting myself organized for the next school day. A little while after the boss left, John said he wanted to talk with me. I quipped, "Well, what marital advice did you give him?" John curtly replied, "It has nothing to do with that."

I do not know about your household, but at our household, when the girls were home, if you ever wanted to talk privately about a matter, you headed to the bedroom. (Even then, I think our oldest daughter had bionic ears!) We proceeded to go upstairs to the bedroom. John informed me that Dow Chemical would be laying off workers, including two salaried chemical engineers. The boss had informed John that he was one of those engineers. When John told me this unexpected news, I just stood by the bed, shocked! At that particular moment, everything seemed surreal to me, and time seemed to stand still. I had little sleep that night.

The next morning, I felt like a zombie going through the motions of getting ready for school, driving to Brazoswood High School, and teaching my classes. I have often said that if anyone has a serious problem or if something is weighing heavily on one's mind, you need to be a teacher because once you step into the classroom, you will not have time to think about anything but your classes! Teaching is demanding, and you do not have a moment to consider personal problems. You are just too consumed with classroom activities and twenty-five to thirty active students. However, once the school day ends, reality sets in again.

Driving home that day, I remembered a book I had read titled *One Man's Healing of Cancer* by Harry DeCamp. It is a personal story about Harry DeCamp, who went to a doctor's appointment only to find out that he had bladder cancer. Then, the doctor proceeded to do exploratory surgery. However, the doctor just sewed Harry up and told him that his cancer was so pervasive throughout his body there was little he could do. At home Harry became so sick that he could not eat very much nor even sleep in a normal sleeping position. His only reprieve was to sleep in a reclining chair in a half-sitting position.

While Harry was home, he received numerous get-well cards and sympathy notes from family and friends, but he also received in the mail a copy of a *Guideposts* magazine. While perusing it, two stories caught Harry's attention. These stories were about a man and a woman who had focused on the Scriptures and were resolute on maintaining a positive mental attitude to help promote personal healing; they consistently visualized their healing every day. The specific scripture that caught Harry's attention was Mark 11:24 (NIV), which says, *"...whatever you ask in prayer, believe that you have received it, and it will be yours."*

Because of his dire prognosis, DeCamp felt that his back was against the wall. In response to reading these two stories, DeCamp began praying healing scriptures over himself, hour by hour, day by day, and month by month. He disciplined himself to think positive mental thoughts about his healing. DeCamp said, *"I ran this picture through my mind hundreds of times every day and night. I talked with God all day and night. I began to feel that I, not the cancer, was now in control. That in itself was a tremendous morale booster*" (DeCamp 1983, 108). DeCamp applied a 100 percent measure of faith, activated by mentally imagining himself totally healed. His prayer routine, scripture applications, and mental imaging went on for three months or so, *hour by hour, day by day—every day—all the time.*

After several months of consistently following this daily routine, one night something dramatic happened! DeCamp saw Jesus walking toward him. In fact, Jesus walked right through him! At that very moment, a warm feeling permeated his body, and DeCamp was instantly healed! In this fascinating book, DeCamp asserted that he knew without a doubt at that very moment that he was healed! This happened late at night, and out of his exuberance, he yelled to his wife a request for a subway sandwich. Because he hardly had had an appetite for several months, his wife thought he was hallucinating.

Like DeCamp, I, too, felt like my back was against the wall. I decided I would follow DeCamp's prayer model. I focused on praying specific scriptures, and I literally became a "praying machine." The key scripture I prayed over and over was Matthew 7:7 (NIV), "*Ask and it will be given to you; seek and you will find; knock and the door will be opened to you.*"

I prayed this scripture constantly at intervals throughout my school day. When the bell rang for a class to be dismissed, I prayed during the five-minute passing time until the bell rang for the next class. When I walked to the Xerox machine to run off class papers, I prayed. When I walked to the front office on an errand, I prayed. At the end of the school day, while I drove home, I prayed. Later, when I stepped into the shower at night, I prayed. I consumed myself in prayer; that is all I did! I constantly and repeatedly prayed that a door would be opened for John's employment.

One day, I was standing by my podium at school, and I sensed that I should ask the teacher across the hall to pray for my family. This teacher was Sandra Moraw Sommerfrucht, the friend I have mentioned several times. At that point I did not know Sandra very well, even though we had both taught English on the same hall for years. Because Sandra taught eleventh-grade English and I taught tenth-grade English, we did not have much opportunity to interact with our subject matter because, essentially, we were teaching two different grade levels and different subject matter. However, because of this "nudging," I walked across the hall to Sandra's classroom; I asked her if she would pray for my family. I had no idea if she even believed in prayer, but I just followed that "nudging" in my heart. I told Sandra that I could not tell her the reason for my request or give any details, but my family needed prayer. As I have already stated, John was not even supposed to know about his pending Dow dismissal. Sandra did not ask any questions; she complied. We sat at students' desks in her room, and she prayed for my family.

During this stressful time, I felt like I had a dark cloud above my head, following me all the time. At that specific time, I certainly could relate to the Peanut's cartoon character, Pig-Pen, who is known for the perpetual cloud that follows him wherever he goes, but regardless of how I felt, I kept praying and speaking into the atmosphere Matthew 7:7 (AMPC), *"Keep on asking and it will be given you; keep on seeking and you will find; keep on knocking [reverently] and [the door] will be opened to you."*

One day at school, I told Sandra that I did not know why, but I had just sensed in the spiritual realm I was hitting a brick wall; however, I continued praying. During the months of March, April, May, and into the early month of June, I continued praying to the Lord, knocking on the door to be reopened for John's employment.

While all this was transpiring, Sandra and I traveled to the Dallas/Garland area to hear Pastor Marijohn preach. At this informative meeting, Pastor Marijohn preached, and then she began speaking prophetically to individuals. Fortunately, I received a prophetic word; Pastor Marijohn said:

> "You are going to begin to discern the tactics of the enemy. And you are going to recognize and take a stand and move him back... But this is some new warfare; some new things have been pressed against you. God is going to give you the enlightenment and understanding to take your stand in Him and pray and see the enemy move back from your household, from your finances, and from the things you put your hands to. It is like there has been thievery and robbery—the enemy robbing and being a thief. That is his job! That is what he does best, but you are going to recognize those tactics, and you are going to begin to stand and say no. The enemy is going to be moved back through your stand."

I kept pondering this prophetic word, and then the realization came to me that the enemy had been working against our family's circumstances and John's job. With this insight and realization, I began praying and pushing back against the enemy using God's Word.

MORE SHAKE-UPS!

At this particular time, another unsettling event happened. Our middle daughter had been home for spring break. When it was time to return to college, she made plans to meet her ride on I-45 in Houston, not far from Humble, Texas. Another college friend, who lived in the Kingwood area, planned to meet Jenny in the Humble area, and then the two of them would connect on I-45 with the third friend, the driver, for their return trip to college. Plans were also made to meet Jenny's friend and her mom in the parking lot of Pappasito's Cantina restaurant in Humble. Then, the four of us would proceed onto FM 1960 to the designated spot to meet their driver. As planned, the mom pulled up into Pappasito's parking area with her daughter and parked next to us. Jenny and I greeted them. I said to the mom, "We can go in my car." The *minute* I said those words, a very strong foreboding rose up inside of me, alerting me that I should *not* drive my car. However, I overrode the warning, and we all piled into our family's new Honda Accord, not quite six months old.

I proceeded to drive west on FM 1960, heading toward I-45 to connect the girls with their ride. I turned left on a green light onto I-45. Out of the corner of my eye, I saw a truck that was approaching the same light but from the opposite direction. The driver had a red stop light, and I assumed he would stop. Within seconds after glimpsing the truck, my daughter screamed, "That man is going to hit us!" Immediately, the truck plowed into the right side of our Honda. The minute the impact occurred, I *heard* an internal voice say very clearly to me, "The devil is in your life!" Then, our car's front window seemed to momentarily pause, as if it was contemplating the truck's impact, and then the glass proceeded to drop all at once straight down, shattering into millions of pieces! There was a moment of dead silence in the car. We all sat there shocked! I guess because I was so stunned, I turned to the mom and repeated to her what I had just heard internally. Looking at the mom, I said, "The devil is in my life!" Then, I thought to myself, *Oh dear, what will this lady think about me?* The mom just looked at me, momentarily wide-eyed with a shocked look on her face, and then she vehemently asserted, "We're all okay! We're all okay!" My strange comment was completely ignored and was not part of any further conversation. She probably thought the car accident had somehow "jarred" my senses and my brain!

The girl's mom questioned the driver of the truck

and said to him, "Didn't you see our car?" The man's only comment was, "I thought you had driven on past the light." Later, our insurance company informed us that our car was totaled!

John was at his mother's home in Humble, Texas, waiting for my return. When I called, John's mom answered the phone. I told her what had happened, and she relayed the information to John. John immediately lamented and said, "That was our new car!" His mother made sure he regained the right perspective; she said to him, "Just be glad no one was hurt!"

Any enlightenment or insight that I experienced during that time always seemed to occur at my podium. At the end of another school day, I was again standing by my podium. At that moment, a strong inner "knowing" rose inside of me, and I knew John had a job. In fact, I knew in my heart that a job would come forth within the next two weeks. This was profound news to me because I had been lamenting to myself every day about the situation. During this stressful time, two of our girls frequently called home to check on how John and I were faring. Our third daughter, the youngest one, was still in high school and home at the time. My sister-in-law also called several times to check on me because I was so emotionally distraught. In fact, my sister-in-law just happened to call that very evening after I had received this "new intel information" by my podium. I quickly related to her that John would have a job within the next two weeks. There was this *long* pause on the phone. She did not know what to think! I had gone from lamenting about our situation to her to being optimistic and positive. I knew John had a job! I am not sure I convinced my sister-in-law about a pending change in our situation, but I knew in my heart John had a job. First Kings 8:28 (NIV) says, "*Hear the cry and the prayer that your servant is praying in your presence this day*," and the Lord was hearing my prayers.

During this family crisis, unknown, of course, to me, the Lord was working diligently behind the scenes. The Lord used an engineer friend of John's to be John's emissary. The friend had flown to Midland, Michigan, which is Dow Chemical's main headquarters, on a Dow assignment. The trail of events and God's hand in this situation are remarkable. As John's friend was walking down the hall of the main Dow building in Midland, Michigan, he just "happened" to run into the former operation manager at Dow Freeport, who had been promoted. He and his family had moved to Midland, Michigan, for his new job assignment. This former operation manager at Dow Freeport and his family had been our neighbors when John and I were first married, so we knew the family. John's friend stopped and chatted with the former Dow boss. He voiced his opinion that he thought John had been unfairly let go at Dow Freeport. The former operation manager replied that he was not involved in that decision, nor was he in charge of that department, but he did tell John's friend that he would see what he could do. Then, the former Dow boss called Bobby. Bobby and his family were also former neighbors. We had all lived in a circular court, close to each other's house. At that time, Bobby was head of Dow Environmental, which was in Houston close to Westheimer. Bobby called John. After some discussion and negotiations, Bobby hired John as a chemical engineer for Dow Environmental, a division of Dow Chemical in Houston.

I was so grateful that I had had a "running start," so to speak, to pray "ahead of the problem." John had lost one job and then was hired for another job at a Dow subsidiary. Life seemed to normalize; John had a job, and I continued teaching at Brazoswood High School.

However, the Lord was not finished with this phase of my spiritual instruction. I always get up early every morning to pray and read the Bible before I start my day. After my prayer time one morning, I decided I needed to water the roses in my front flower bed. I stepped outside, went to the faucet, turned on the water, and lifted the hose to begin the watering process. As the water began flowing, I distinctly heard the Holy Spirit speak to me! The Holy Spirit said, *"I closed that door to get your attention! I closed that door to get your attention!"* I was so surprised upon hearing those words that I screamed and simultaneously flung the water hose wildly about in the air. I ran into the house and called Sandra, sharing with her what had just happened because I was so astonished at hearing the words, "I closed that door to get your attention!"

Later, reflecting on this episode, I realized the main scripture I had been praying to the Lord over and over was Matthew 7:7 (AMPC), *"Keep on asking and it will be given you; keep on seeking and you will find; keep on knocking [reverently] and [the door] will be opened to you."* I had been asking, seeking, and knocking that the door be reopened for John's employment. I pondered those words that I had heard, and after a while, I realized that the Lord had closed the door to John's employment at Dow Chemical—*to get my attention*! *Why?* I was so comfortable in my routine, my job, my family, and my life in general. God had to shake things up! Those words, "I closed that door to get your attention!" were a call from the Lord to walk more closely with Him. Have you noticed in your life sometimes how the Lord will use a traumatic situation or a difficult circumstance to get your attention!

JOHN'S HEALTH ISSUE

During this time our middle daughter graduated from college with a computer analysis degree and was hired by a company in the Dallas area, where she met her husband-to-be. They planned a September wedding. Three weeks before their wedding date, John commented that he felt several lumps on the side of his neck; he pointed them out to me. I felt the knots under his skin. Of course, I did not know what to think. Then, the wedding was upon us. Family and relatives converged in the Dallas area for the festivities. John mentioned the lumps on his neck to his sister, a pathologist who lives in New Mexico. She examined his neck and told John he should have a doctor check it out.

After all the wedding activities, we returned home. I made an appointment for John to see Bruce, a doctor friend of the family. Prior to John's appointment, our oldest daughter had a dream. In her dream she had seen John completely bald. She shared with me that she just knew in her heart that the lumps on John's neck were cancerous. Simultaneously, our youngest daughter also had a dream; she, too, saw her dad bald, but this time John was standing with his back to her. (At that time John had more hair than now!) The oldest and the youngest girls were surprised that they had similar dreams, so they called their middle sister, thinking she, too, might have had a similar dream. They were disappointed that their middle sister had not had a similar dream too.

For me I did not have a dream, but I did have a keen sense of foreboding, a feeling that the nodules were cancerous. Just thinking about the situation made me upset, and I told John about my apprehension. He laughed and said, "Here you're telling me I have cancer, and I have not even seen the doctor!" The appointment day finally arrived; our doctor friend, Bruce, did the biopsy, and the report came back that the nodules were indeed cancerous. He talked with me in his office about the negative biopsy report. I was not really surprised because of the girls' premonitions and my foreboding. I distinctly remember that my only response to the discussion as I sat there was to say, "It's going to take a lot of prayer." That is all I said. I was not shocked because the Lord had prepared me ahead of time for the news.

Several days later, I sat down with John, and I told him that I did not know how or where, but he was going to get into a Bible class. I told him that he needed to know God's Word. I was not sure what to do, so I called Bruce because I remembered he had mentioned to me that his church was planning to start a Bible study program. He commented that John was welcome to come to his church, but he mentioned a non-denominational program called Bible Study Fellowship that was being organized in our area. He told me to call another friend of the family, another doctor friend, who was involved in helping to organize the Bible study. I knew John would not just show up on his own for the start-up class, so to get him there, I told him I would go with him. The Bible study meetings were to be held at the Presbyterian Church. We went to the first meeting but were told the actual start-up date would be the following Tuesday, *but* it was only for men. They informed me that a women's group would be meeting separately during the day if I was interested. I realized this women's Bible study group was the same one I had attended before returning to teaching.

So the following week, John attended the Bible study class—this time alone. On returning that first evening, John walked into the house and declared, "I like the

Catholic Church. I like the music. I like everything about the Catholic Church!" Then he added, which revealed what was really bothering him, "Those guys are just one step away from being preachers!" I realized John was really saying, "I'm not comfortable. I'm out of my comfort zone!" At that point, I asked the Lord, "Lord, what do I do?"

Thirty minutes later, I received a phone call from a friend. She told me that she now worked at our local hospital, and she had just typed John's medical report that very day, so she was calling to check on me. In fact, this friend had been in the women's Bible study group with me. I explained to her my plight and John's reaction to his first meeting. She sympathized with him and said she understood exactly how he felt; she said she had felt the same way when she began attending the women's Bible study group. She advised me to tell John to try it for a little while. So I followed her suggestion. After her phone call, I went to John and asked him to try the Bible class for a little while, and I added, "Try it for me."

John complied and began attending the Bible classes. There were eight groups in all. Fortunately, John was placed in his doctor friend's group, so this helped to ease his discomfort. Our doctor friend also asked John to be his "roll taker" at the meetings. So now John had a purpose; he was the "official roll taker." The Bible class assigned extensive homework questions that accompanied all the readings.

One day, I came home from teaching, and John was so frustrated; he did not know the answers to some of the questions and was exasperated. I told him I would help him. We began the weekly routine of reading the questions, discussing the answers, and writing them down. During the men's Bible class, every man was called upon to answer a question or questions. When John returned home, he would give a report about how many times he was called upon, his response, and how he thought he did.

John reached a point where he relaxed in the class. He even admired the man who had the responsibility of preaching to all the men after the close of each class session. While attending the classes, John told me he wished he could sneak me into the meetings so I could hear this man preach because John thought he was so good. John stayed in this Bible study group for eight years. Each year, they studied a different book of the Bible.

AN UNTRAVELED ROAD
PART 1

John attended his weekly Bible classes, and simultaneously he had pending doctor appointments. After the biopsy, our local hospital completed the medical report about the biopsy. We made an appointment with the oncologist at our local cancer center in Lake Jackson. After our initial visit, the oncologist ordered various tests for John. A teacher friend covered for my classes on the first day of medical tests; however, it reached a point where I just had to get back to my classes. While I was walking back to the car, memories of John's dad's hospital experience flooded my mind. I remembered John's dad lying almost motionless in bed, very sick with prostate cancer. I recalled him saying, "John, I didn't think you would ever see me this way." So there I was, walking back to the car, reflecting on those words. I had just left John hooked up to all these numerous wires. Though the words were different from his father's, John said to me, "I can't believe I'm here. I can't believe this is happening to me!" I seemed to be walking down a familiar path.

A day or two later, Sandra, my good friend, took it

upon herself to call Pastor Logan and tell him about John's medical report. It was just as well that she did because I would have become upset just talking about it. The following Sunday at the end of his message, Pastor Logan asked those individuals who needed a healing touch to step forth. I stepped forward as a stand-in for John. Pastor Logan prayed for individuals, and when he approached me, he said, "If you can believe...just believe!" He continued and said, "Speak and stand against the spirit of death and destruction over your household. The Lord is very merciful and long-suffering toward you and your soul mate. The blood is over your house."

Those words encouraged and strengthened me.

The next week on September 28, 1997, I was driving to church and listening as usual to the KSBJ, a Christian radio station. The pastor who came on KSBJ every Sunday morning at that time gave his Sunday message. As I drove to church on that Sunday morning, this pastor was teaching 1 Kings 17:5 and discussing the widow woman who was experiencing a storm in her life. The pastor said we all have storms in our lives. He went on to say that one minute we experience joy in life, and the next minute there is a phone call, and things change. I thought to myself, *Boy, isn't that the truth!*

We had just celebrated Jenny's wedding with joy and laughter, and now we received the news about John's biopsy. The pastor on the radio then asked, "What do you do in a storm?" He replied to his own question and said, "You prepare." He went on to say that our preparation in a storm is to use the Word of God. As I drove along, he continued his discussion about the widow woman's plight. At that specific moment, I felt like the Holy Spirit was using this pastor on the radio to speak directly to me about my family and the dire situation we were experiencing.

Then, at church Mrs. Bascom's Bible lesson for the week focused on becoming established in God's Word. Later, Mrs. Bascom spoke to the congregation, also referring to 1 Kings 17:5 and the widow lady! She said the widow lady did not have much confidence in her situation, so she said to her son, "We will prepare this last bit of bread, and then we'll die." Mrs. Bascom discussed another passage in the Bible about the widow lady where her son appeared to be dead. The prophet Elijah, however, miraculously brought her son back to life. Mrs. Bascom went on to say that the widow lady walked through all these storms in her life, but she continued to have faith in God. What was happening? The Holy Spirit was using Mrs. Bascom to speak to me about the widow lady, her plight, her problems, and how she coped with the issues in her life, but she continued to have faith in God.

Then, Mr. Bascom came forth to call for the offering. Mr. Bascom gave a short message saying that we should have confidence in God and get to know Him. He said to talk to God about your concerns and say, "Lord, here are my needs." He added, "If you know God, you'll have confidence in Him. You won't have confidence in God if you don't know or don't believe in Him." The Holy Spirit was speaking to the congregation, *but* the Holy Spirit was also speaking to me using Mr. and Mrs. Bascom.

Then, Pastor Logan preached the Sunday sermon. His theme was to develop one's faith, and he focused on Exodus 14:9, where Pharaoh and his soldiers pursued the Israelites. Pharaoh, his men, and all their chariots came rushing after the Israelites, but the Egyptian soldiers drowned in the Red Sea. Pastor Logan declared, "Throw all confidence to the Almighty." He said, "Just focus on the Almighty." He added, "Don't throw away your confidence; believe God," and he reminded everyone that we do have an enemy. He said you thought to yourself, *I've tithed, gone to church, loved God, walked in obedience, and then there was this attack.* He further stated, "And you are saying to yourself, *What did I do to deserve this!*" (The Holy Spirit was reading "my mail.")

Pastor Logan proceeded to quote John 10:10 (NIV), asserting, "*The devil comes only to steal, kill, and destroy...*" and he reminded everyone there would be opposition in life. He further asserted, "This is not the time to throw your faith away. The enemy is after your faith. It's faith in God that moves mountains." Pastor Logan continued, "You need to set your emotions aside and just wait on God." He added, "Don't doubt and forgive others." He then quoted Matthew 7:7 (AMPC), "*Keep on asking, and it will be given you; keep on seeking, and you will find; keep on knocking [reverently], and [the door] will be opened to you.*" Pastor Logan had no way of knowing that Matthew 7:7 was a scripture verse that I was quoting and *knew quite well!*

So, on this Sunday morning, the Holy Spirit used a pastor's message on KSBJ radio, Mrs. Bascom, my Bible teacher, Mr. Bascom, a deacon in the church, and Pastor Logan, the minister of the church, to instruct me to exercise my faith, stand, and continue to persevere in spite of John's negative medical report.

AN UNTRAVELED ROAD
PART 2

The following week, John and I had another appointment with the oncologist in Lake Jackson. The doctor discussed the possibility of chemotherapy as a treatment. John told the doctor he wanted to think about it and decide what to do. He requested a copy of the hospital's medical report so he could send it to his sister, the pathologist. John wanted his sister's opinion about the matter. When his sister received the hospital's analysis, she said she found inconsistencies in their findings in comparison to the biopsy report. She thought the analysis and the report did not line up with each other. Then, she suggested that John should go to MD Anderson for a second opinion.

On the following Wednesday evening, I attended church. Before the service began, Pastor Logan came to me because he was concerned about John's health and the issues we were facing. I informed Pastor Logan about John's sister's recommendation. He agreed and encouraged us to go to MD Anderson. He commented, "Well, I think the Lord is directing you to go to MD Anderson." He added his concern and sympathy, but I told him not to give me too much sympathy because

I would begin to focus on the problem, get upset, and start crying, and then I would not be able to talk to him. On the following Sunday, Mrs. Bascom came and sat down beside me before the church service began. She, too, was trying to comfort me. I shared with her that "Everyone thinks they have faith, but when you are really faced with a difficult situation, you begin to wonder if you really have faith in your heart to endure and preserve."

You never know how you will react when faced with a difficult dilemma in life or how you will react to a negative medical report. Also, you never know who the strong person in the family will be to strengthen everyone else. I would like to say that I was the strong one in the family or that the girls were the strong ones or that we were all strong, and that we all supported John, but the fact of the matter was John was the strong one in the family who emotionally supported all of us! He was always the stronger one; he was always saying something to strengthen us and help us cope with the unknown road ahead of us, and he was the one with the health issue!

On Sunday, October 1997, John agreed to go to church with me. Because he was reared in the Catholic Church, I was apprehensive about how comfortable he would be in a different church setting. Before service began, Pastor Logan happened to walk into the sanctuary. He momentarily stopped because he noticed John sitting with me. He then proceeded to walk over to Diane, his wife. He said something to her. Diane always led the singing and the worship team. Next, Pastor Logan motioned to Mrs. Bascom, and he also spoke something to her. Mrs. Bascom left the sanctuary and returned with some hymnal books for the worship team to use. When the worship service began, the worship team sang several songs from the hymnal book and a few other songs they usually sang. At that moment I realized that Pastor Logan had changed the whole worship service for one person—my husband. Why? So that John would feel comfortable in the service.

Pastor Logan preached his message, and at the end of the service, he asked for all who needed healing to come forth. Along with others, John and I walked forward. When Pastor Logan came to us, he opened his Bible to Psalm 23 (NIV) and read:

> The LORD is my shepherd; I lack nothing. He makes me lie down in green pastures, he leads me beside quiet waters, he refreshes my soul. He guides me along the right paths for his name's sake. Even though I walk through the darkest

valley, I will fear no evil, for you are with me; your rod and your staff, they comfort me.

When Pastor Logan came to verse 5, he stopped, looked at both of us, and continued, "*You prepare a table before me in the presence of my enemies. You anoint my head with oil; my cup overflows.*"

Pastor Logan then added, "Jesus is the healer. He is the bread of life!" Then, he said to us, "If you can, just believe!" The Lord was speaking to our hearts, telling us to have faith and to hold onto His Word.

There was another incident where the Lord used a pastor to speak to me. One Sunday in December, Sandra and I again attended Pastor Janette's church for a Sunday evening service. At this particular service, Pastor Janette spoke a word to me and said, "The Lord is forming a miracle before your eyes. You will see miracles for holding on." The Lord was trying to encourage and give me strength as John and I faced the unknown future, this cancer, and the medical experiences we would walk through at MD Anderson.

Not long after that, I happened to be home alone on a Saturday without any family members. My family was here and there and involved in other activities. I was alone in the kitchen. The house was quiet without the usual chatter of activities. I just stood there for several moments in the kitchen, and then I told the Lord that if I did not have His Word to hang onto, I did not think I could make it. I also added that money did not mean anything to me, my home did not mean anything to me, but now my family, I told the Lord, "That means something to me."

The very next day was Sunday, December 6, 1997; I went to church as usual. We had a visiting evangelist as the guest speaker. He knew nothing, of course, about John's medical diagnosis. Near the end of his message, he walked over to me, paused, and said, "The enemy has attacked you from all sides. He has brought all sorts of things against you. Things even look impossible to believe, but out of the simplicity of your faith, you said, 'Lord, I believe.'"

Again, what had happened? The Lord was reassuring me that He had heard my conversation with Him the day before in my kitchen. Those spoken words were very comforting to me. Jeremiah 29:12 (AMPC) says, *"Then you will call upon Me, and you will come and pray to Me, and I will hear and heed you."* I had called upon the Lord, and the Lord had heeded my call about John's health. He was confirming His Word and strengthening me spiritually for what lay ahead.

MD ANDERSON

MD Anderson does not accept medical tests and reports from other hospitals. They do their own tests no matter how many tests were performed by another hospital, so John had some of the same tests, some new tests, and extensive blood work authorized at MD Anderson. The medical conclusion was similar. John had enlarged lymph nodes in his neck, plus some were also found in his abdomen area on some of the medical markers. Because the doctors were evaluating and trying to narrow down John's specific type of cancer, we made numerous trips to MD Anderson. In fact, we made so many trips for John's analysis that I began to recognize some of the cancer patients.

The first specialist we saw about John's case was a lymphoma doctor. He informed us about the various types of lymphoma cases he treated. He told us that his cancer patients usually have between five to eight years to live. He also said they would inject John with some type of radioactive material to see if his heart valves could take a shunt for chemo treatments. He added that he was studying all the perimeters and aspects of John's case to see if John qualified to be one of his patients. However, after several visits, this doctor said that

John's test results and symptoms did not line up with all the criteria and markers for the type of lymphoma he treated. He referred us to another doctor who was located on the sixth floor.

We made an appointment with the cancer specialist doctor located on the sixth floor. After numerous visits, various meetings and discussions, plus even more tests, John was diagnosed with Waldenstrom macroglobulinemia. Waldenstrom is a rare blood disease with only about 1,500 cases per year in the US, and it occurs more frequently in older adults. It is the type of cancer that affects two types of B cells and white blood cells. Long term this type of cancer can cause one's eyesight to diminish, and it can damage organs in the body. Essentially, a person's blood gets "clogged" with bad protein cells, and this clogging interferes with normal organ functions in the body, and the results of all of this: body organs can shut down and even cause blindness because of all the "clogged pipes."

The doctor discussed John's tests and the meaning of all of them, and he handed John a copy of the report. John requested a copy to be sent to his sister, the pathologist. A week or two later, we returned for another office visit. During this second office visit, John asked the doctor if he would call his sister while we were in his office because she had some questions about the medical report and she wanted to discuss John's case with him. The doctor picked up the phone and called. While sitting and listening to their conversation, I kept praying for a clear understanding of John's diagnosis and for wisdom as to how to proceed. The two doctors had a long conversation. They did not come to a complete agreement about John's case because there were so many complexities to it, but John's sister finally conceded to the doctor's analysis and recommendation, stating he was the Harvard graduate with training in that specific medical area.

Immediately after this visit, John and I headed for a scheduled patient counseling session. The counselor inundated us with all types of papers and information—parking information, insurance stipulations, billing payments, papers, papers, and more papers. Sitting there listening to the counselor speak, I became emotionally overloaded. We had been to doctor after doctor, visit after visit, tests after tests, and I reached a point where I just sat there, emotionally drained, distraught, and overwhelmed with the circumstances: the constant trips to MD Anderson, the various medical tests, the constant analysis of possible types of treatments, and the endless discussions about a specific diagnosis. I sat there extremely tired and distraught, and tears began to form in my eyes. The counselor just kept talking, trying to avoid looking at me, I'm sure, but finally, he reached a point where, I guess, avoidance was not an option; he handed me some Kleenex tissues. John, always the strong one, continued as a participant in the conversation while I sat there "cratering," unable to speak. John was the one who had the medical problem, but I was the one cratering. John was the one who was showing strength and fortitude in the face of a medical dilemma; I was the one experiencing an emotional meltdown. I'm sure the counselor was glad to see this emotionally distraught lady leave his office.

The first thing the doctor prescribed was Interferon shots for John. John had to have these shots in his stomach because that was a good location to find some fatty tissue. John, a chemical engineer, was very proficient in the lab, and he did not trust me, the family cook, to find the measurement line where to draw the Interferon into the syringe, so he measured and fixed the syringe himself. I became, out of necessity, a nurse because it was hard for John to look down and give himself shots in the fatty tissue of his stomach. It is a wonder he trusted me to give him the shots. He certainly did not trust me in a lab situation. Within thirty minutes after receiving an injection, John became extremely ill; he felt exhausted and tired. He described the feeling as if you have a very, very bad case of the flu. Then, John had to lie down and wait until he regained some strength to continue his day. This procedure and process went on every day for a year. Finally, the doctor decided that Interferon was not helping John, so he discontinued its use.

During this time at the high school, the bracelets WWJD (What Would Jesus Do) were popular with the teenagers who loved the Lord. I noticed several students wearing them in class. At one point during one of my English classes, I stopped and mentioned to the students that I noticed some of them were wearing the WWJD bracelets. I asked them to please pray for my husband and his health problems. I did not elaborate; I just asked them to pray for my husband.

On another day in another English class, I also requested prayer for my husband with students who were also wearing the WWJD bracelets. However, on that day, I did not remain as strong as with the other class. I became momentarily upset as I requested prayer for my husband. That evening, our high school held its annual open house for parents to meet the teachers. While visiting with the parents of one of my students, the mother mentioned the fact that her son had become concerned about me because I had become upset in class. Just mentioning the subject was too much for me. Tears started welling up in my eyes. All I could say to the student's parents was, "The Lord is going to heal my husband." Then, I turned to get a Kleenex from my desk. Of course, the parents did not know what to say, and they left the classroom as I was reaching for a Kleenex tissue.

One morning, before classes began, I stopped by Becky's room for a short visit. Becky was head of the English department and had substituted for one of my afternoon classes when I had accompanied John to MD Anderson. She asked about John. I gave an update, and she looked at me and said, "Rosamond, those doctors don't know you are a bulldog." I looked at her and said, "Yes. You are right." That was Tuesday. The next day, on Wednesday evening, I went to church. The youth pastor happened to be preaching the evening service. The title of his message was "Hang on Tight!" At one point during his sermon, the youth pastor paused and then interjected into his message, "You hold on tight just like a bulldog! You get your teeth in there, and you hold on!" I felt like the Holy Spirit was tapping me on the shoulder, speaking directly to me, saying,

"You do that!" I sat in the service, thinking, *This is the second time in twenty-four hours that I have heard those same words.* The Holy Spirit's message to me was to persevere and hang on tight in the days ahead, no matter what we had to face.

On the following Sunday morning, Pastor Logan began the service reading Isaiah 40:21 (NIV), which says, "*Do you not know? Have you not heard? Has it not been told since the beginning...*" and Pastor Logan paused and finished the sentence with, "That I am God." Pastor Logan then spoke to the congregation and said, "This is a word for someone here." He looked around and asked, "Who is it?" I raised my hand. Pastor Logan looked directly at me and prayed that the feelings of weariness would be lifted off. Again, the Lord was strengthening and reassuring me to hang on tight. Before the Sunday evening service began, Kathy, who is now with Aglow International in Washington State, came over to me, put her hand on my shoulder, and prayed for me. Kathy told me that she just sensed in the spirit that I needed more prayer.

TRIALS AND TRIBULATIONS

We continued our many trips to MD Anderson. John's blood had to be drawn and analyzed every three months, plus there were numerous follow-up visits with the doctor. There were also additional trips for frequent CT scans to measure the size of the enlarged nodules on John's neck and in his abdomen area. John, however, did not have any fever or night sweats that often manifest in individuals who have Waldenstrom. John continued these medical visits and tests four times a year for six years. Over those many years, the size of the nodules stabilized and did not enlarge.

Because his data and numbers did stabilize, John was able to talk the doctor into letting him come every six months instead of every three months for tests and evaluations. Then, much later, as time progressed, the doctor also agreed to extend John's evaluation visits to once a year instead of every six months. Around this time, MD Anderson began using PET scans instead of CT scans for analysis, reports, and medical decisions. With a PET scan, a liquid is injected intravenously as a radiotracer to measure and find cancer cells in the body. In John's case, the PET scans were used to measure the size of the nodules in his neck and abdomen area. The blood tests, of course, continued along with the PET scans.

On October 10, 1998, we experienced another medical problem. While I was at school, my neighbor across the street called me before one of my classes and began to tell me that his wife had taken John to the hospital's emergency room. Our neighbor had had a stroke, so he was not able to drive John to the hospital. This call naturally upset me because I did not know what was going on. Later that afternoon, the neighbor called me again to tell me that John had returned home. When I arrived home, John said the air conditioning ducts in our family room began to swirl round and round, and he could not stand up. He said he crawled to the phone and called our neighbors across the street. While at the hospital, John's dizziness finally subsided. The hospital wanted to do more tests, but John said he wanted to wait and see if the dizziness returned, so the hospital released him. This incident, of course, weighed on my mind the rest of the week.

On the following Sunday morning, a group of ladies and I were praying prior to the morning service. At the end of our prayer time, Kathy Sanders, whom I have mentioned before, came over to me and said that she just sensed that I needed prayer. She prayed such a "right on prayer" that she brought tears to my eyes. Isn't it amazing how the Holy Spirit works? Kathy did not know anything about John's dizzy spell that week or anything about my concerns about this new medical problem. Kathy was just being sensitive to the Holy Spirit's leading.

Like Kathy, Pastor Logan did not know anything about John's dizzy spell. At the very beginning of the service, Pastor Logan read Isaiah 40:21–22 (NIV), saying, *"Do you not know? Have you not understood? Has it not been told since the beginning? Haven't you understood since the earth was founded? He [God] sits enthroned above the circle of the earth..."*

Unaware of my week's experience with John's health issue, Pastor Logan looked up, directed his eyes toward me, and said, "That scripture is for you." He also prayed for physical and spiritual strength for me. Pastor Logan and Kathy were obedient servants to the promptings of the Holy Spirit, bringing peace and comfort to me because of my difficult week.

The Lord cares about everyone. My situation was not any different from anyone else who experiences problems or health issues. I was just grateful that Kathy and Pastor Logan were sensitive to the Holy Spirit and obeyed the promptings of the Holy Spirit to strengthen and encourage me. Proverbs 25:11 (AMPC) says, "*A word fitly spoken and* in due season is like apples of gold in settings of silver. "Those words were definitely "*apples of gold in settings of silver*" for me at that time.

John's medical problems continued. A year later, on October 11, 1999, I was attending church, and Pastor Logan began the service reading Isaiah 59:19 (NIV), saying, "*For when the enemy come in like a flood, the Spirit of the Lord will put them to flight.*"

Pastor Logan then began to flow in the prophetic and said to me:

> "'Even I am going to cause you to go into My storehouse,' saith the Lord. 'I will cause you then to pull out grace and mercy in the time of trouble. For when the enemy comes in as a flood, My Spirit will lift up even a standard against the very enemy of your household...the very enemy that would cause death and bring death. Amen. My grace will rise up. My Spirit will rise up. As you focus and as you look and as you look away from the bad reports, the negative reports, and as you begin to look unto Me,' saith the Lord. 'Amen. I will begin to even take the weariness off of you,' saith the Lord... 'Even the enemy would try to bring doubt and even bring defeat. Amen. I will

cause him to move on. Amen. I will defeat him.
I already have,' saith the Lord.

"'Amen. Now it is your turn; it is your part...
to look and to see the grace and the mercy;
amen, that is in the storehouse for you. Draw
it out,' saith the Lord. 'That grace will enable
you, and that grace will cause strength. When
others around you are negative and others
around you are defeated and others around
you are wanting to give up, your faith will
begin to blossom. Your faith will begin to
grow. Amen, for I am the author and the
finisher of your faith,' saith the Lord."

Pastor Logan then added, "Hallelujah. Hallelujah.
Hallelujah. Hallelujah. Hallelujah. Thank God for
His presence."

One of the purposes of prophecy is to encourage
individuals. Pastor Logan's words certainly encouraged,
strengthened, and helped me to rise above my
circumstances and weariness. I read those prophetic
words over and over during those difficult days; those
words were a tremendous comfort to me.

The scheduled medical tests continued, and the
doctor continued giving us copies of John's results, his
data sheets, and the charts diagramming the results.

One of the diagrammed charts plotted John's B2 macroglobulin serum tests. This serum test measures the amount of protein called beta-2 macroglobulin (B2M) in the blood, urine, or cerebrospinal fluid. B2M is a type of tumor marker, which is a substance made by cancer cells or by normal cells in response to cancer cells in the body. At the beginning of testing, John's B2M numbers were high and remained high for quite some time, but in 2005, John's B2M numbers began to track somewhat downward. The graphs showed a slow, steady decline over time with an occasional blip up, and then the diagram line would start tracking back down again for the succeeding months; one could see on the overall graph line a continuing decline on the chart.

John's immunoglobulin IgM numbers were also plotted and diagrammed on another graphed chart. This test measured the antibodies in his blood. Antibodies are part of the immune system, which responds to viruses, fungus, or cancer cells in the body. John's numbers were extremely high, but over an extended period of time, years, in fact, these numbers eventually began to track downward. By July 29, 2004, John's IgM numbers were down 14 percent from his original 1998 high numbers. In 2004, John's medical report also stated that the enlarged nodules in the abdomen area had decreased somewhat from their original enlarged size. Nodules found in other areas of John's body remained stable. The most positive aspect of the report was that the nodules had not increased in size. We were encouraged!

Whenever we arrived home from these doctor visits, the first thing John did was to take the medical data sheets and plot the data and the numbers on a computer program he had built on our computer to track his numbers.

ANOTHER MEDICAL DILEMMA

Two years later, in May 2006, John was using a long pole cutter to trim some pecan trees in our front yard. He gave the rope a strenuous yank to snap off a high tree limb. The moment he yanked on the rope, he heard a pop and simultaneously felt severe pains shoot through his right forearm. This occurred near the end of my school day while I was organizing for the next day's lessons. John called and told me what had happened, so I packed up my papers and immediately came home. We then went to an emergency care center. They took an X-ray, which showed a fracture of the bone of his right arm and a smaller splintering of some bone near the same area.

The next day at school, I shared with Sandra what had

happened and the subsequent visit to the emergency care center and the results. Sandra told me that I was certainly holding up well and being strong about this latest medical problem. I told her that the Lord had strengthened me along the way because of all John's health issues. I also told Sandra that I felt like I had been down this road before; in fact, it seemed to be a familiar road.

Because John was being treated at MD Anderson, we decided it was best to return to John's doctor concerning his arm problem. John had to wait a week or two for an appointment, so he improvised a sling to hold his arm steady and in place. He had to make sure he kept his arm steady because he experienced pain at the slightest movement.

The appointment day finally arrived. John told the doctor a month or so before the arm injury that he had had intermittent discomfort in his right arm whenever he moved it. The doctor ordered an X-ray. The X-ray revealed a pathologic fracture of the right ulna, and there was also a small lytic lesion of the right radius. A pathological fracture is a broken bone that is caused by a disease rather than some type of bodily injury. Somehow, John's cancer had weakened the bone in his forearm. In his medical report, the doctor stated that the presence of lytic bone lesions in Waldenstrom's disease was highly unusual, so he ordered a fine needle aspirate by an interventional radiologist to study the cause. Lytic bone lesions are spots of bone damage that result from cancerous plasma cells built up in the bone marrow. Because of the plasma cell blockage and build-up, bone cells cannot break down and regrow as they should. Thus, bones become thin and create an abnormal "hole" in the bone structure. John had several holes in the bone structure of his arm.

Because this was so unusual, the doctor ordered additional bone surveys for John's whole body to see if there were other areas where his bones had become thin and had "holes" in them. He also ordered a bone marrow aspirate to check the status of John's bone marrow and see what type of blood cells were being produced in his body.

Things sometimes do not always go as planned, and for some reason, the medical lab botched John's biopsy specimens. In this specific case, the biopsy specimen was contaminated with a lot of blood along with some debris; thus, the pathologist did not have a good, clean sample to analyze and arrive at any clear conclusion as to the cause of John's fractured arm. The doctor then scheduled for John to have an appointment with a radiologist.

THE RADIOLOGIST AT MD ANDERSON

The weekend before John's appointment with the radiologist, Sandra and I drove to the Dallas/Garland area to hear Pastor Marijohn preach. Traveling to the meeting, I had a heavy heart. Pastor Marijohn was one of those special people who ministered in love. Her words were always uplifting, and she spoke comforting words to individuals. As always, she preached and then ministered prophetically to individuals.

At one point while speaking, Pastor Marijohn turned and said to me, "The Lord says, 'I'm with you; I'm for you, and you're not alone.'" Although additional words were spoken to me, those words, "I'm with you; I'm for you, and you're not alone," strengthened and helped me in this situation.

The following week, John and I drove to Houston for the first appointment with the radiologist to discuss the radiologist's plan to restore bone loss and promote healing in John's arm. As we walked down those long halls to the appointment, I kept repeating to myself over and over those words that were spoken to me, *"I'm with you, and I'm for you, and you're not alone."* Those were comforting words that I treasured in my heart, and I kept saying them to myself as we walked along.

We passed many offices and hallways we did not even know existed at MD Anderson. This was a part of MD Anderson we had never seen. As John walked along, his arm kept radiating pain. He was using the sling apparatus he had devised, but he had trouble keeping his arm steady and stable.

Finally, we found the office. The radiologist discussed with us her plan to remediate John's injured arm. She explained the goal of radiation was to break up all the blocked, clumped cells at the injury site so blood could once again flow, thus promoting bone restoration and healing to the forearm. She prescribed radiation therapy: One radiation session per week for twelve weeks. A special cast had to be made so John could slip his injured arm into the cast for the radiation treatments.

When John finished his twelfth radiation treatment, he had one last set of instructions. The nurse instructed him to ring a special bell, a tradition in the department that signified a patient had completed all his radiation treatments. Before leaving, John asked if I could see the radiation room. The nurse complied. What I remember most about that room was the innumerable wired helmets hanging everywhere all over the wall. The helmets were configured to the shape of each patient's head. By following these procedures, the radiation treatment would be precise and locate the exact spot to kill tumor and cancer cells.

After completing the radiation treatments, John was given the name of an orthopedic surgeon at MD Anderson. We made an appointment to see this doctor for the final assessment of the forearm bone. After three appointments, the doctor told John that the bone in his forearm was healed.

THE CONTINUATION OF TREATMENTS

John continued his regular trips to MD Anderson for blood tests and other specified tests. As time went on, John asked the doctor if he would extend the time even more with his tests and appointments. Because test results were showing John's cancer to be stable, the doctor agreed.

I was not able to accompany John on every office visit because of my teaching responsibilities at school; however, I do remember one conversation John related to me after a doctor's appointment. He said on this visit the doctor had said to him, "I have had cancer patients whose numbers continue to rise on the chart, but I have never had a cancer patient whose numbers gradually go down on the chart." John replied, "My wife says it's because she's praying for me." The doctor paused and then said, "Could be."

THE NEW DOCTOR

Eventually, John's doctor at MD Anderson retired, and another doctor who specialized in that specific field of medicine took over the retiring doctor's practice. On the first appointment with the new doctor, we had to wait quite a long time in the examination room. The doctor finally entered the room and told John he had spent considerable time studying his files, tests, and background information. Then, he did a quick physical check on John. He ordered various extensive medical tests plus the usual blood tests. Later, we returned for an appointment to review the analysis of the blood tests and all the tests. We received the printed data with graphs that, by this time, were quite familiar to us.

In 2012, John received a surprise. His IgM numbers were the lowest they had ever been. Because John's IgM numbers were so much better, John discussed with this doctor the possibility that his appointments and tests could be extended to a year and a half. The doctor agreed.

In 2016, the doctor ordered a PET/CT scan to evaluate and update all of John's records. There were not any outstanding changes, and John was given copies of all the medical reports.

A GOOD REPORT

In 2019, a PET/CT scan was used to compare the results with previous PET/CT scans. The doctor discussed the results with John. With a smile on his face, the doctor told John that his cancer had been arrested, and, based on the recent test results in comparison to previous test records, John was cancer-free! Yippee! No more appointments to MD Anderson. No more PET/CT! No more blood tests! No more apprehensive moments while waiting in the waiting room area, crowded with many people who were also waiting to have their names called by their doctor's nurse.

One scripture I repeated over and over to myself through all the years John was a cancer patient at MD Anderson was Psalm 41:3 (NIV), which says, "*The Lord* sustains them on their sickbed and restores them from their bed of illness." This scripture materialized before our eyes.

I have shared with the reader that when we were just beginning this unknown walk concerning John's cancer diagnosis and medical problems, Pastor Logan had said to us, "If you can just believe, the Lord will instruct you." At that time, we were instructed to keep our eyes on the Lord and not the problems.

Pastor Janette had also prophesied that "a miracle is forming before your eyes." At the time she spoke those words, we were just beginning the trials and tribulations of John's medical issues. However, now that we have come through all those difficulties, I can look back and say, "Yes, indeed, the Lord performed a miracle before our very eyes!"

AN ADDITIONAL MEDICAL CONCERN

Besides being a patient at MD Anderson, John was simultaneously a patient at Houston Methodist. Cancer cells had been found in several areas of his prostate. After undergoing an examination and a biopsy, John and I returned for a scheduled appointment with the urologist. The urologist recommended robotic surgery to remove John's prostate. The urologist's decision was based on the pathologist's report of finding perineural invasion in John's prostate. Perineural invasion is when cancer cells invade and grow along the nerves. The doctor explained the details for the procedure and the extended recovery time and the cautionary warnings.

John's response to the urologist's recommendation for robotic surgery was that he would think about it. He also asked permission to have his biopsy slides sent to his sister, the pathologist, so that she could have an opportunity to study and analyze John's slides. I thought the removal of John's prostate was the best answer to the problem because John would not have to ever worry about cancer in his prostate. Because John's father had died of prostate cancer at the age of fifty-seven, I was in favor of the robotic surgery. I thought this surgery would solve John's prostate problems.

A few weeks after the appointment with the urologist, we visited our youngest daughter in Austin. While visiting, I attended Arise Ministries' conference. Dr. Hamon, along with his team of Christian International ministers, were the speakers. They also had several prophetic teams organized to minister to individuals. I signed up for prophetic ministry. So here I was in Austin at a Christian conference, and the lady who prophesied to me, of course, knew nothing about John's health problems, his prostate prognosis, or the doctor's robotic surgery proposal. She was one of the ladies on staff at Arise Ministries. Prophecy is amazing. The prophetic team member gave me this remarkable prophecy. An excerpt of this word stated:

"God says, 'Do not hold on to the word of the doctors and the things that are spoken but hear My word.' 'Hear what I say in this situation–physically–what I'm saying for that situation because I have the final word,' says the Spirit of the Lord. 'And I am the Great Physician, and I will bring forth the miracle. I will bring forth the answer. I will bring forth the remedy, but I will bring it forth quickly, but I will bring it forth in My time for My situations to shift to cause everything to get into alignment. When the physical ailment leaves, the spiritual alignment will come forth,' says the Spirit of the Lord. 'You will be a witness to that, and you will begin to share that it was Me that did the work. It was Me that caused the breakthrough.'"

So, of course, after receiving this word, I "shut my mouth" about any suggestion that John should undergo radical robotic surgery. Think of that! Those were words I had spoken only to John; no one else had heard those words but the Lord! The Lord answered me very clearly and directly what I should do–*speak only words of life*!

THE MYSTERIOUS A2 SLIDES

After returning from Austin, John contacted Methodist Hospital to make sure the biopsy slides had been sent to his sister, the pathologist. Methodist employees assured John that they had been sent. John's sister received the A2 slides. While studying them, she did not find any perineural nerve invasion, so she asked three other pathologists who worked and collaborated with her to look at the slides and give their opinions. They agreed; there was not any perineural invasion on the slides. John's sister then discussed the situation with the other pathologists. Puzzled, John's sister kept saying to herself, *Have I missed something? How could our analysis be so different?* After pondering the problem, John's sister realized that if there was a set of A2 slides, surely there had to be a set of A1 slides.

Then, John's sister called the pathologist at Methodist in Houston who had examined the slides and written the report. After some discussion with him, she asked the pathologist if there was a set of A1 slides. Sure enough, there was. In unraveling the mystery, she learned there had been a total of thirty slides; John's sister had only received fifteen slides, the ones labeled A2. The Methodist pathologist agreed to send the A1 slides. We drove to Houston so John could pick up the set of A1 slides and send them to his sister. When John picked up the box of slides, he double-checked the box before we left the Methodist Hospital parking area. Irony of ironies, he had been given the same set of A2 slides again! John immediately called Methodist, explained the mix-up, and returned to obtain the box of A1 slides.

Eventually, John's sister received the box of A1 slides. The results: yes, there were perineural cancer cells on these slides. A pathologist who worked with John's sister and knew about John's situation suggested that he should go to Johns Hopkins in Baltimore, Maryland, for a second opinion; he said there was a doctor on staff who was well-known for his work on prostate cancer. The pathologist even suggested that John should call him. So John called the doctor's office. Expecting to speak to a secretary, John was surprised because the doctor himself answered the phone; he was extremely helpful. He informed John that Johns Hopkins Hospital set aside a time in the fall and in the spring to review cases with a panel of doctors. Then recommendations were made based on each person's medical issues. He was so gracious; he even looked up the phone number that John needed to sign up for this health evaluation program, which took place at Johns Hopkins' Prostate Cancer Multidisciplinary Clinic. John called the phone number and signed up for the program. We then made plans to fly to Baltimore, Maryland.

Prior to the trip, the Johns Hopkins health program had numerous papers for patients to fill out. John filled out all required medical papers to be studied by the panel of doctors. The panel also requested John's pathologist's report, prior medical reports, and the set of A1 slides from Methodist.

JOHNS HOPKINS MEDICAL CENTER BALTIMORE, MARYLAND

We had never been to Baltimore, Maryland. We took the subway for our early morning appointment. While traveling on the subway system, we kept seeing on the subway walls poster after poster stating, "If you see something, say something!" These warning posters were everywhere. The atmosphere in the subway was heavy and daunting. When we went above ground to the sidewalk level, men were loitering near the subway station, on the sidewalks, in front of stores, and just about everywhere as we walked to the Johns Hopkins meeting. You did not feel safe! John has a good sense of direction, so I followed him. Exiting the subway, we proceeded to walk toward Johns Hopkins' Sidney Kimmel Comprehensive Cancer Center. When we arrived, the meeting was just getting underway. We joined three other couples who were there for their medical assessments too. We met in a small conference room. A nurse explained general information to all attending, and we were given a packet of introductory material. Everyone was assigned to a patient diagnostic room. John underwent various examinations by a nurse and then a doctor. This took up all morning.

We were free for the afternoon, so we walked around the Baltimore area near the waterfront. We spotted a police officer standing nearby, directing the flow of traffic. We had seen the Baltimore riots on TV just a few weeks before, and we mentioned the riots to the policewoman. She said she had been on duty that day, and she commented that a lot of teenagers were involved in the turmoil. After listening to her observations about the riots, we asked her the best place to eat. We took her advice and ate at an Italian restaurant. Later, we planned to visit the aquarium on the waterfront. We were trying to decide the best time to visit the aquarium–afternoon or evening–but the ticket person advised us that the afternoon was the best time to go. She strongly advised against being in the area after dark. She said it was not safe. We followed her advice and bought an afternoon ticket. The next day we flew home.

Several weeks after returning home, we received Johns Hopkins' report. The doctors agreed with Houston Methodist's report that there was perineural cancer invasion on the nerves along John's prostate. No further information was given, so John double-checked Johns Hopkins' website for any further instructions. The website said that suggestions for any medical action would be given based on findings. Nothing else was stated. John called his sister. John's sister suggested that he should call Johns Hopkins to see if there were any recommendations for his specific case. John thought it would be difficult to get anyone to answer the phone, but he complied and called. The doctor who had read and analyzed John's slides was the *very person* who answered the phone. The doctor was helpful and told John that prostate surgery does not necessarily mean the cancer problem would be solved. He explained that surgery might not solve the problem because perineal nerve invasion was located along the nerves, and he said because of this fact, cancer cells could return. He did not recommend prostate surgery for John, and his advice to John was to not do anything. He said medical research was now suggesting that men who have cancer cells in their prostate should not have surgery. In fact, the doctor said John might die of other things before he died of prostate cancer.

Chapter Four

ALL THOSE THINGS IN THE AREA OF MINISTRY OTHERS WOULD LOVE TO HEAR ABOUT

THE HOLY SPIRIT AT WORK

Jesus said, "Because if I do not go away, the Comforter (Counselor, Helper, Advocate, Intercessor, Strengthener, Standby) will not come to you [into close fellowship with you]; but if I go away, I will send Him to you [to be in close fellowship with you]."

John 16:7 (AMPC)

Eight months after our first child was born, I returned to teaching. However, whenever I dropped our daughter off at the babysitter's house, I always felt guilty about leaving her. Four years later, when our second child was born, I was able to stay home with our two girls. Around this time, I began pondering the idea of attending graduate school. My friend, Jackie, who lived in Lake Jackson at that time, told me that it was much easier to go to graduate school when your children were young rather than when they were older. She said later children become involved in various activities. So, acting on her advice, I decided the best time to attend graduate school was while the girls were very young.

I also had a friend who had an elementary degree with a specialization in reading. In my discussions with her, I realized that there were many children, for whatever reason, who had reading problems and needed extra help in order to be successful in school. I decided to get a master's degree as a reading specialist. My plan was to get a master's degree, test and evaluate students' strengths and weaknesses in reading, tutor them, and thus ameliorate reading and learning difficulties.

About this time, I became pregnant with our third child, but I proceeded with my plans to attend graduate school anyway. My friend helped me analyze degree requirements at the University of Houston's main campus versus the degree requirements at the University of Houston at Clear Lake. Essentially, we found the course selections at the two schools were similar, so I chose to enroll at the University of Houston at Clear Lake because there was less traffic and travel time. I also decided to take nine graduate hours every semester so that I could complete the degree requirements in two years.

Online computer registration was not available at that time. So I found myself standing in a registration line, pregnant and wondering if I could really do this. Could I go to school three nights a week, handle all my responsibilities—a husband and two children with a third child on the way—and find time to study? I kept pondering those questions, so one evening I asked my husband, "Do you think I can take nine hours each semester?" But I was really saying, "Will I be able to drive two hours (round trip) to the University of Houston at Clear Lake, attend classes, study the assignments, take tests, and manage all my responsibilities at home?" John answered me matter-of-factly and rather nonchalantly. He said, "You can do it." That was his answer: "You can do it!" Proverbs 16:24 (AMP) says, *"Pleasant words are like a honeycomb, sweet to the mind and healing to the body."* John's answer, "You can do it," were *pleasant words* to my soul; they were reassuring and encouraging words to me. I kept repeating those words over and over to myself the first week of classes. I kept telling myself, "You can do it!"

By this time, our oldest daughter was in first grade, our second daughter was beginning nursery school, and the baby was due in March. I kept repeating John's words to myself, "*You can do it*," as I organized my days. Time went by quickly, and I completed the first semester. Then, I enrolled in the second semester, again taking nine semester hours and attending classes three times a week. Because my due date was in March, I planned ahead, completing as many assignments and written papers as possible before my March deadline.

During that time, I learned that the mothers in my neighborhood were concerned about my driving back and forth to class three times a week as the time approached for the baby's arrival. In fact, the baby's deadline shifted, and the baby was due earlier than the date the doctor had predicted. This was not in my plans! I had one more test scheduled for the following Monday that I wanted to complete before delivering the baby.

Saturday morning, prior to Monday's test, I went to the gynecologist for my final examination. I told the doctor that I wanted to take one more test before the baby's arrival. He said the only way I *might* make it work would be to stay in bed the complete weekend. Hearing that, I gave in because I would still need to drive to the University of Clear Lake on Monday, attend class, and take the test. I doubted that I could make it. He admitted me to the hospital that day. The baby made her entrance into this world rather quickly that afternoon.

So now, with the new baby, I adjusted my study routine. While our second child attended nursery school in the mornings and the newborn slept, I studied. Around noon our second daughter arrived home from nursery school, and I fixed lunch, fed the baby, changed her diaper, and put her back to bed for an afternoon nap. Then, I read books to our daughter before her afternoon nap time. While those two napped, I studied. In fact, one evening, as I left for class, I told John, "You keep that baby up so she will sleep during the day while I study."

This plan worked quite well—too well, in fact! One day, I picked the baby up to change her diaper; she looked at me and began to cry. She probably wondered, *Who is this lady?* Then, John picked her up, and she became quiet. We did this several times back and forth. We laughed about how well my study plan had worked.

TESTING AND TUTORING STUDENTS

When I completed my master's degree, I began testing students, analyzing their reading abilities, and initiating a remediation program for each one. I never advertised. I was inundated with requests from parents to help their child. Word of mouth was my sole means of advertising. My students were comprised of all grade levels: pre-kindergarten, kindergarten, elementary, intermediate, and even some students on the high school level. Sometimes kindergartners were behind in their readiness skills. Other elementary students often lagged behind because their maturation rate was on a different schedule than the school's schedule. These students just needed some extra time and individual help. Other students needed to improve their reading comprehension skills; others needed help in deciphering words. I was busy; I tutored after school every day and sometimes even on Saturdays. I tutored year-round for eight years, helping students become better readers along with their improvement of other skills. It was gratifying to see students gain confidence in themselves and in their school assignments.

One of my fondest memories was the opportunity to tutor a high school boy who was ambitious and determined to do something with his life. Somehow, he had missed some reading skills. I tutored him for over a year. He had tremendous self-drive, and in one of our conversations, he said to me, "I'm going to make something of myself." He graduated from high school, took classes at Brazosport College, and later transferred and graduated from the University of Houston. Years later, I ran into him, and he told me he really appreciated what I had done for him. I replied, "You were a diamond in the rough, just waiting to be discovered."

AN UNUSUAL EXPERIENCE

As time progressed, our three girls attended three different schools—elementary, intermediate, and high school. When our oldest daughter was in the ninth grade, we began experiencing a new phase in our family dynamics—the teenage years. Some parents go through the teenage years with various trials and tribulations; other parents escape what can be very frustrating and dramatic years. Our family, however, was not in that fortunate category. We experienced a lot of struggles, drama, and first-hand "teenage resistance."

During this stressful time, I had an unusual experience. Our youngest daughter was in first grade at that time. Like most moms, I carpooled. On one of my carpooling days, I thought to myself, *I have a few minutes before I leave to pick everyone up, so I will clean the utility sink*. I began to vigorously scrub the sink, and suddenly the globe-shaped light fixture, which was positioned directly above my head, broke loose and fell across my right hand. The moment the light fixture hit my hand, I immediately heard the words, "The devil is in your life!" I stood there, stunned! The cut looked ugly, and blood began oozing out. I called another carpooling mom to see if she could pick the children up. During our conversation, I mentioned to the mom about hearing a voice say to me, "The devil is in your life!" As I conversed with the mom, we both agreed that this unexpected interjection was really nothing and I should ignore it. So I ignored it. The cut on my hand was bleeding a lot, so I thought perhaps I might need stitches. I called Mary, who lived down the street at the time. I asked if her husband, a doctor, would be able to look at my cut. She said this was his day off, but she would call him. She called me back and said to meet him at his office. At his office this kind doctor and family friend placed several stitches on the cut to stop the oozing and bleeding.

However, the interjection, "The devil is in your life," proved to be quite true in our family at that time. Because of the "teenage resistance" we were experiencing with our oldest daughter, our family was in constant turmoil. At the onset of this resistance, my friend Jackie advised me to go to His Love for counseling so that we would be equipped to handle all the dynamics happening in our family. During that tumultuous time, John quipped, "It is too bad when your children turn thirteen that you can't just put them in a closet and bring them back out when they turn twenty-one." His Love's counseling service was our rescue haven, helping us navigate through those difficult times.

At this time I was attending a women's Bible study program, which I'm sure was another reason I had heard the interjection, "The devil is in your life!" I was reading and studying God's Word, and the opposition did not like it.

A RETURN TO THE HIGH SCHOOL

When our youngest daughter was in third grade at Beutel Elementary, I needed to drop off an item for her at the school's office. I just happened to run into Brazosport Independent School District's history supervisor. She had been my supervisor when I had taught history. Approaching me, she said, "When are you returning to the classroom?" I really had not thought too much about returning to teaching because

I was so busy tutoring students. The moment, however, when I heard her question, I experienced what I can only describe as some type of a *reverberation*; some type of *alarm* went off inside of me! It is hard to describe the experience, but it was like a wake-up call went off inside of me. Whatever it was, I had never experienced that type of alert before! The history supervisor proceeded to tell me about a pending vacancy in the history department at the high school. She informed me that Dow Chemical was transferring a teacher's husband and his family to the Netherlands for a two-year stay. She proceeded to tell me that the vacancy would be in American history. This was a subject I had previously taught.

Later, reflecting on our conversation, I realized the history supervisor had not greeted me with the usual, "How have you been?" or said to me, "What have you been doing?" Her first words to me were, "When are you returning to the classroom?" Proverbs 16:33 (AMPC) says, "*The lot is cast into the lap, but the decision is wholly of the Lord [even the events that seem accidental are really ordered by Him].*" Of course, I did not realize it at the time, but I can only surmise that this meeting had been ordained by the Lord.

Responding to the prompting of this "wake-up

call," I made an appointment to see the principal at the high school. Prior to my stay-at-home time with my children, he had been my principal. I met and spoke with him about the pending job. Then, I walked across the street to Brazosport Independent School District's administration building and filled out an application for the pending history position.

The next thing I did was pray about this job. At that time I read a book published by Moody Press that spotlighted well-known people of integrity and godly character who had experienced difficulties and challenges in their lives, but they had relied on God's Word and their faith to help them through those trying times. Every person in the book had an interesting story, and they all stressed the importance of praying God's Word. In this fascinating book, a suggestion was made for individuals to write scripture on three-by-five-inches cards that applied to the situation they were experiencing, and then the book instructed the reader to pray using those scripture cards. So that is what I did. I wrote out pertinent scriptures on three-by-five-inches cards. I walked every evening for exercise, so while walking, I talked to the Lord about the pending substitute job, read my scripture cards out loud to Him, and prayed about the job. While praying and walking,

I told the Lord that I wanted to be at the high school so that when my girls were there, I would be there too. I also told the Lord that I wanted to know what was going on in their lives so that when they came home from school and talked about their school day, I would also know what had transpired. I prayed and walked along, reading and using those cards day after day.

One afternoon at 2:30 p.m., I was sitting on the sofa in the family room, praying about the substitute position, telling the Lord again my desire to be at the high school with my girls, and just talking to Him about the situation. After a few minutes of praying, I clearly heard the Holy Spirit say to me, "*You have the job*!" I paused for a minute, then got up, and repeated to myself, "I have the job!" The next morning, because of this "inside information," I thought I should call the assistant principal, Beth, and inquire about the substitute position. I had previously worked with Beth, so we knew each other. When I phoned and asked her about the history position, she replied, "I really can't tell you anything; it's up to the principal." So I thought to myself, *Well, I will just have to wait and see what happens*. However, early the next morning, Beth called me back and told me I had the job. Reflecting on the sequence of events and the Holy Spirit speaking to me at exactly 2:30 p.m., I can only speculate that Mr. Marcum finalized his decision to hire me at exactly 2:30 p.m., when I had heard those words in my spirit, "You have the job."

While substituting at the high school, I continued my discussions with the Lord, continually reminding him about my desire for a job at the high school. Whenever I went to the office on an errand or whenever I walked to the Xerox room, I talked to the Lord. I told Him, "This is where I want to be—at this high school—with my girls as they progress through high school." I continually prayed and talked to the Lord about a permanent position for the upcoming school year; my substitute job was only from March until the end of the school year in May.

The school year ended, and summer began. The summer months progressed, and I continued my routine of walking, praying, reading my scripture cards, and talking to the Lord about a permanent position at the high school. During this busy summer, I continued tutoring students in reading and helping them in various ways. One morning in July, I was tutoring a fifth-grade boy. I had given him a silent reading assignment. I quietly sat next to him, waiting for him to finish the reading so we could proceed with the lesson.

While sitting there, I suddenly received an urgent *SOS* ticker-tape message from the Holy Spirit! This was an incredibly unique message because I saw this SOS message travel across the front part of my brain. I clearly saw a ticker tape banner with the message, *"Call Mr. Marcum! Call Mr. Marcum!"* It just moved across the front part of my forehead. That is the only way I know how to describe this unusual occurrence.

I finished tutoring the fifth grader and fixed lunch for the girls. While eating lunch, I kept pondering the message I had just received. At the end of lunch, I said to myself, *Well, I had better act on this!* I called Mr. Marcum to see if a teaching vacancy had occurred. He said, "No, I wish I had a spot for you because I would hire you." Then, I asked him if it would be okay if I contacted the personnel administrator for Brazosport Independent School District. He said, "Sure, go ahead." I immediately called the personnel director, gave my name, and inquired about a vacancy. His immediate response was, "The principal has hired you. A teacher in the English department resigned this morning and is moving to Austin; she signed her leave of absence papers this morning." Surprised, I questioned him, "Does Mr. Marcum know this?" He said, "Sure! He said when there was a vacancy, he wanted to hire you." Then I asked him, "Is it okay if I call him about this matter?" He said, "Sure. Go ahead!" I immediately called Mr. Marcum a second time and repeated to him everything the personnel director had said to me. When I finished speaking, there was a long pause on the other end of the line, and he said, "Let me get back with you." I waited for a phone call the rest of that day, but he did not get back with me. Then, I waited two more days, but I did not hear from him. I finally said to myself, *One way or another, I need to know if I have the job or not.* I called the principal a third time; I did not get a chance to say anything but my name because he immediately interjected, "Your assignment is ninth-grade English," and he proceeded to tell me my class schedule. He had forgotten to call me back to tell me I had the job!

THE HIGH SCHOOL

I taught ninth-grade English at the high school for several years, and later I was "promoted" to tenth-grade English. On the first day of school in one of my English classes, a tenth-grade boy walked by my desk. I looked at him, and without even thinking, words just tumbled out of my mouth, and I said to him, "I know you don't want to be here, but it is going to be all right!" Surprised at my words, he stopped momentarily and then proceeded to find a desk. A few minutes before the end of the class period, I spoke to this student and asked him where he was from. He told me he had moved here to live with his grandparents because he had gotten into trouble at the other school. He was upset because he had left his friends. There was another interesting moment in that same class. A few days later, students were sitting according to the seating chart so I could learn their names. Checking roll, I turned, and I just happened to look toward my left. There were two boys sitting on the same row; one sat in the middle of the row, and the other boy sat near the back. I looked at them. To the boy sitting closest to the front, I said, "I look into your eyes, and I just see some sort of sadness or deep darkness in your eyes." To the other boy sitting in a seat near the back on the same row, I mentioned to him that I saw a similar type of sadness/darkness in his eyes, but it just did not have the same intensity as the other student's. Later in the school year, the boy who had had the deep darkness/sadness in his eyes was working at a pizza place in Lake Jackson; I stopped to buy a pizza, and he took my order. I brought up the subject about the day I saw that darkness/sadness in his eyes. He said, "Yea, that was one of my bad days." He never explained to me any details about his bad day, but what he does not know is that while in my class, I had prayed for him and whatever was occurring in his life at that time.

THE DOCTOR'S APPOINTMENT

One summer, I had an appointment with my gynecologist in Houston for an annual check-up. During my early prayer time on the day of my appointment, thoughts kept coming to me about my gynecologist. He was a friend of the family. John's dad, who had been a doctor, had collaborated with him on numerous cases. While driving to Houston for the appointment, I received a strong impression that I should pray for him. At the appointment he examined me and gave me some instructions. Sitting there, I silently said to Lord, "How will I ever have an opportunity to pray for this man?" *At that very moment, his phone rang.* Before answering the call, he turned and instructed me to meet him in his office. Later, I sat down in his office, and he gave me some medical instructions, and when he finished speaking, I told him that I felt like I should pray for him. Raising his voice, he said, "Me! Pray for me?" He quickly added, "I'm having all sorts of problems!" Words tumbled out of his mouth. He said, "The IRS has requested files and records way back," and he added that he was also having problems with his office staff too. He said he had asked some nuns to pray for him. I got up, walked to his side, and put my hand on his shoulder. He was a short Italian doctor like John's dad, so it was easy for me to put my hand on his shoulder. He had such a reverence for the Lord; he bowed his head as I prayed. I had never done anything like that before, but the impression in my heart was so strong that I prayed for this man.

A few weeks later, Sandra and I drove home from a weekend ministry event; I had been praying in the Spirit. Then, the Holy Spirit downloaded to me a mental picture. In the spirit realm, I saw the top of the doctor's filing cabinet covered with blood, and the blood slowly moved down the sides and covered the entire cabinet. I surmised that this blood was symbolic of the blood of Jesus. I can only assume from this impression that the inquiry into his files and records had been lifted and the matter had been resolved.

THE FLEA MARKET

When our middle daughter was attending North Texas University, she wanted to go to a popular flea market in East Texas while we were there. We drove to this flea market. We walked around looking at the various booths, and we came upon one booth that was selling back massagers. Stress and tension always seemed to linger in my neck and shoulder area, so I was interested in looking at the product. However, as I approached this booth, I immediately sensed something was wrong. I turned to my husband and asked him, "Do you feel like something is not quite right here?" He just looked at me and replied, "No." I repeated to him what I sensed, and I again said, "Something is not quite right." I had some birthday money, so I overrode my negative feeling and said, "Okay, I will buy the massager."

Later, when we returned to our daughter's apartment, John's leg began bothering him because of all the walking we had done; he got out the massage machine to massage his leg. As the massage balls began rotating, John felt something sharp and rough on his leg through the fabric covering the rotating balls. Curious, John unscrewed the four screws that held the massager machine together and discovered that one of the rotating balls was half-broken, plus dust had accumulated around both balls. John realized this was not a new machine!

So the next day we had to drive back to the East Texas flea market to find the man's booth. Finally locating it, we learned the man had taken a lunch break, and we had to wait for his return. The man finally arrived. John showed him the massager and the exposed broken ball section; the man did not say a word. He just refunded our money. My lesson on that day: I should have listened to the Holy Spirit's prompting!

THE PERSIMMON TREE

At a Sunday service, a visiting minister, Pastor Stephen, preached a message, and then he began prophesying to individuals. I was one of those individuals. He prophesied to me that I would see a spiritual sign in my home. We often wait years for a prophetic sign or prophetic word to come to pass. However, this word of knowledge materialized quickly.

My next-door neighbor informed me that a man who lived near us had cancer and was extremely ill. I shared this information with Sandra, my friend; we decided to go to the man's house and pray for him. In the meantime, the Lord connected his family to my family in a unique way.

John is an avid gardener and fruit tree grower. In our front yard, he had planted a persimmon tree that he "babied" and inspected every day. Eventually, it began producing persimmons. One day, the lady whose husband had cancer had a free moment and a break from taking care of him. She was walking along and spotted John's persimmons on the tree, and she proceeded to pick some. Ironically, my husband pulled into the driveway at the same time. Much to his dismay, he spotted the lady picking his "precious persimmons" that he inspected every day. Of course, incredulous at what was taking place, he walked over to the lady. She immediately told him that her husband had cancer, and this was the only thing he would eat. On hearing this, my husband said, "Take the whole tree; take all you need." Then, he helped her carry the fruit in a box to her house. While there, my husband shared about his father's bout with cancer and his eventual death. Before beginning our dinner meal, I prayed for the sick man, his health, and his family. When I finished praying, I looked up and saw tears in our youngest daughter's eyes. The Holy Spirit had touched her heart; I realized this was the sign that had been prophesied that I would see.

AN ELDERLY PARENT

One Sunday evening, Pastor Stephen returned as a guest speaker at the church. At one point during the service, he stopped and said, "There is someone here who is taking care of an elderly parent in their home. Would that person come forward?" I thought to myself, *I have an elderly parent, but I'm not taking care of him in my home. My father is in a nursing home.* Then the pastor added, "Perhaps this parent is in a nursing home." Then, I did step forward. He asked me if my father had been saved. I told him, "I do not think so." He said, "Just keep praying for him."

A WEDNESDAY EVENING SERVICE

A few months later, Pastor Stephen was again a guest preacher at the church, but this time, he spoke on a Wednesday evening service. I had invited two boys from my English class to the service, and I called their parents to obtain their permission. The evening service continued until 9:00 p.m., and at that point, I became concerned about getting the boys home because it was a school night. When I saw an opportunity to leave, I picked up my purse and Bible and motioned to the boys to begin walking toward the door. Pastor Steven, however, stopped speaking and said to one of the boys, "Young man, come here." Feeling responsible for the student, I walked with him to the front, and the pastor spoke a prophetic word to him. The main thing I remember him saying was, "You can go to Hawaii, or you can go here, or you can go there, but wherever you go, the prayers of the saint will follow you." The speaker also told the student, "You're walking down a dark lonely path."

After class the next day, Jose stopped by my desk to talk with me. I said, "Jose, who is praying for you, your mother?" He immediately replied, "No, my grandmother." I had typed his prophetic word for him, and I gave it to him.

Later, he told me that he had shared the typed words with his grandmother. The student was puzzled about the meaning of his word, but the grandmother explained it to him and helped him understand it. So, you see, God honors our prayers. This grandmother had been praying for her grandson. A few weeks later, I learned that at that particular time in Jose's life, he had been contemplating joining a gang. I surmised that the thought of joining a gang was the "dark, lonely path" that was alluded to in Jose's word.

THE BROWNSVILLE REVIVAL

Sandra and I, along with her two sons, attended the Brownsville Assembly of God Revival in Florida. Revival evangelist Steve was used by the Holy Spirit to ignite the Brownsville revival on Father's Day, June 18, 1995, at the church. The pastor of the church said that his church had been praying for two years during their Sunday evening services for a move of the Spirit and for a revival. Their prayers preceded the revival. It did not just happen. The congregation had prayed and prayed, saturating the atmosphere with prayers and declarations for two years, and then the Holy Spirit moved upon the scene.

Sandra's son was the youth pastor at our church at that time. Evangelist Steve was the scheduled speaker at the church on that weekend. He was scheduled to speak to the youth on Saturday morning. Sandra and I accompanied her sons to the Saturday morning session. After delivering his message, evangelist Steve began walking around the large room. He did not go near anyone, but when he was about twenty feet from the students, they started falling under the anointing of the Holy Spirit. It was like a button was pushed, and they began falling. This was not a flaky thing. The students were taken by surprise, and it was the most astounding thing to witness. I thought to myself, *He is like a lawn mower, spiritually touching the teens without even going near them.* I watched and intently studied him as he walked along. It was fascinating to watch the Holy

Spirit move. The evangelist was like a steam roller. He never touched anyone! He was not near any youth! Then, he made a turn to come down to the side where we were standing. I thought to myself, *I'm just going to stand here and watch what happens as he walks along.* The evangelist was at least fifteen feet or so from me, and without even realizing it, I fell down. Everything happened so quickly. I can only relate this experience to the one described in the book of Acts, where Peter began speaking to the crowd, and then everyone spontaneously began speaking in different languages. What we all witnessed with the evangelist was a spontaneous movement of the Spirit touching people.

Several years later, the pastor of the Brownville Assembly of God Church was a guest speaker at First Assembly of God in Brazoria, Texas, on a Sunday evening service. Sandra and I attended the service. The guest pastor preached his message and then instructed everyone to turn and pray for someone near them. He began walking among the people, praying for them. I turned and prayed for someone, and then I stood and watched the visiting pastor as he walked about the room. When he came within twenty feet or so from where I was standing, I began involuntarily to back up. I could not help myself; I was just compelled to back up. It was a reflexive action because of the saturation and the anointing of the Holy Spirit. A wave of the Holy Spirit preceded this pastor as he walked about the room. While I was involuntarily backing up, I must have caught his attention because he glanced my way, stopped, and then walked over to me. He put his hand on my forehead and prayed for me. At that moment, the anointing was so strong that I blurted out, "I don't know if I can stand it." He replied, "It is okay." It is hard to describe that moment, but there was such a strong anointing of the Holy Spirit on this visiting pastor.

THE PERIODONTAL VISIT

Pastor Nathan was a visiting pastor with a prophetic gifting; he was the invited speaker at a church service in Freeport on Sunday evening, May 2002. One of the students in my Bible history class invited me to the service. Dolores, a friend, and I attended the service. After the pastor's message, he gave some prophetic words to individuals, including Dolores and me. When he approached me, he asked if I was praying about something concerning my physical body. I replied, "Yes, several areas." He then said, "The Lord is saying that He is going to touch you in your physical body...praise God. Father, in Jesus' name, I pray for a healing and a touch,

Father, in this life, in Jesus' mighty name. Amen."

Several months later, I had an appointment with my periodontist. One of John's brothers was a dentist, and he recommended that I see this periodontist. Much to my dismay, the periodontist scheduled me for gum surgery. On the day of surgery, he placed numerous shots in my mouth to numb all the areas where he was going to graft new tissue in the problem area. During the whole process, I kept my eyes closed. I did not want to see anything because it was such an ordeal to me.

While in the dental chair, I focused on saying to myself Philippians 4:13 (AMPC), which says, "*I have strength for all things in Christ Who empowers me [I am ready for anything and equal to anything through Him Who infuses inner strength into me; I am self-sufficient in Christ's sufficiency]*." However, during the oral surgery, I focused on the portion of Philippians 4:13 that says, "*I have strength for all things in Christ... Who infuses [me with an] inner strength...*" I just kept repeating that scripture over and over to myself during the whole procedure. When the periodontist finished, he commented that I should be awarded a gold medal because I had been his best patient.

About a week or so later, I recalled the prophetic word the pastor had spoken to me about the Lord healing my physical body. It was at that point that I realized the Lord had touched my physical body while in the dental chair; this was my healing. I realized that I had felt absolutely no pain from the numerous shots placed in my mouth to prepare for the gum surgery and grafts.

ANGELS: NORTH, SOUTH, EAST, AND WEST

A group of ladies and I had been meeting and praying weekly at our church for our two co-pastors. The five of us were together on one occasion, praying, and at one point, I closed my eyes. I immediately saw our church's husband-and-wife pastoral team walking along; they were both suited up in what looked like astronaut suits. I saw a small, narrow tube on the right side of their space helmets where they were receiving an inflow of oxygen into their space helmets and body suits. I distinctly saw four angels positioned north, south, east, and west of them, walking closely next to them. The east and west angels were walking along, continually turning and adjusting a small wheel-like instrument, guiding and directing their steps, keeping them on a straight path. The north and south positioned angels were walking, one in front and one behind them, guiding them as they walked along.

Several months later, I attended a Christian conference in Humble, Texas. A lady and her husband were sitting next to me. I shared with the wife what I had seen in the spiritual realm concerning the pastors. The lady turned to her husband, who was also a pastor, and then she turned back to me, and she asked me to repeat my story to her husband. Upon hearing the story again, the lady asked me, "Did you tell your pastor?" I said, "No." At that time I had not said anything, but following the conference, I did share what I had seen in the spiritual realm with my pastor. After listening, he commented, "We have been going through a challenging time."

Why did the Holy Spirit show me this impression? Our co-pastors needed prayer, and the Holy Spirit alerted our group to this spiritual need while we were praying together in our group. We were made aware that angels were guarding their steps. Psalm 34:7 (AMPC) says, *"The Angel of the Lord encamps around those who fear Him [who revere and worship Him with awe] and each of them He delivers."* The Lord was honoring His Word with His angels guarding the path of these pastors.

TOUCHING HEARTS

John and I were planning to go to Plano, Texas, to visit our middle daughter and her family. Prior to visiting our daughter, we planned a meeting in the Dallas area with my high school friends, Adele and William, plus Adele's father. Over the years, William had developed lung cancer; he was under a doctor's care. He did not begin smoking until his late twenties, but he was one of those unfortunate people who did develop lung cancer because of smoking. The doctor administered to William all the chemo and medicines he could, and the doctor eventually told William there was not anything else he could do for him.

Before our planned meeting, I had spent some time in prayer about our visit because I was not sure about William's salvation. During one of my prayer times, I received a strong spiritual impression: I saw all of us sitting together at a round table, holding hands.

On the day of the meeting, we all agreed to meet at a Soup & Salad eatery. The Soup & Salad place was very busy and noisy. Soup & Salad is buffet style, and we served ourselves and sat down at a large, round table to accommodate everyone. I anticipated that we would pray over our meal *before* we ate, but everyone was chatting, and it was just very, very noisy. I said a quiet prayer over the meal, and then I silently said to Lord, "I don't know when I will have the opportunity in this noisy place to pray for William." We stayed a long time, reminiscing, visiting, and chatting. Eventually, the crowd thinned out. The atmosphere became much quieter and not so hectic. Unlike in high school, I noticed that William had become a sensitive person to other people's feelings. He said that he went out of his way to encourage people or tell others, "Thank you," for the smallest things they did. He told me that he and Adele had recently eaten at a restaurant, and he sought out the manager to tell him that the server had done an excellent job serving them. He added, "A year ago, I would not have noticed those things or said anything to anyone."

I do not remember how I introduced the topic about praying for William, but when I said I wanted to pray, everyone automatically clasped the next person's hands as if they had rehearsed the event! It was an instantaneous impulse! The Lord had shown me this very scene during my prayer time! Then, I prayed a prayer, but my intentions were really to pray for William's salvation. One year after our visit, William died. I hope William either knew Christ or accepted Christ on that day when we all met for dinner.

A SCHOOL MEETING

At the end of a school year, I drove our middle daughter and her friend to band camp in Huntsville, Texas. While driving home, I prayed about a parent meeting scheduled for the following Monday at our high school. This student had not put out much effort in class, and I theorized to myself that the parent wanted to question how his grade was computed. While driving home, I kept praying about the pending meeting, and I received the impression that I should go back and refresh my memory about the steps I used to calculate his grade. You would think when I arrived home, even though it was late, I would have immediately checked his grades in my grade book and refreshed my memory. *Well, I forgot*! Because I forgot, I was not fully prepared for the Monday morning meeting with the parent and the assistant principal. During that early meeting, I had the student's papers and tests, my grade book, his class folder and previous classwork, and the boy's final grade, but I became flustered. I could not recall the specific steps and calculations to arrive at the final grade. The assistant principal kept talking to the mother while I kept looking through my papers and grade book. The mother kept responding to the assistant principal's questions and conversation. Near the end of the meeting, the mother accepted her son's grade. However, I should have listened to the Holy Spirit! The Holy Spirit had forewarned me to be prepared!

A HEALING

Sandra and I, plus a few other friends, made a trip to attend Pastors Sandie and Mickey Freed's Friday night service, which at that time was in Bedford, Texas, a suburb of Dallas. I drove, but because our Acura had a recall notice on it, the dealership had lent us a loaner car. I was so concerned about being a careful driver because of the loaner car that I unconsciously tensed up my muscles. As a result, I developed a piercing pain in my right shoulder, and a tension knot developed in that area. We arrived for the evening service. At the beginning of the service, Pastor Mickey called forth anyone who was having back trouble. Several people, including myself, walked forward. Pastor Mickey then went to each person and prayed for them. When he came to me, he instructed me to turn and twist to the right and turn and twist to the left, which, of course, I did. Then, he placed his hand on my forehead and prayed for my healing. When I returned to my seat, I continued to feel a warm sensation on my forehead, exactly where he had placed his hand. This warm feeling remained on my forehead for about ten to fifteen minutes. In bed that night, I kept repeating to myself, "My shoulder area is healed; the muscle knot is gone. The piercing pain has been eliminated." The next morning, when I woke up, I was free of all pain! I did not have a muscle knot! Afterward, I realized the warm sensation on my forehead was a sign that the muscle knot and pain would dissipate.

A POEM

In December, right before our youngest daughter was to graduate from A&M, the Holy Spirit "downloaded" to me a poem about her. One morning at 5:30 a.m., as I was coming out of my sleep, thoughts began swirling in my head. I jumped out of bed, rushed to grab a pen, and then quickly wrote down those thoughts. After jotting them down, I stopped, read what I had written, and realized I had written a poem about our daughter. A few minutes later, John came to the game room and said, "What are you doing?" I replied, "The Holy Spirit gave me a poem about Shelley!" Since it was not an emergency and nothing drastic had occurred, John just looked at me and returned to bed. Later, I thought if I had been in a race to see who could write a complete poem in one minute,

I am sure I would have been the winner!

Later that evening, I shared my poem with John. He listened, looked at it, and pointed out two stanzas that did not rhyme together. I said to him, "I don't know what else to do." Soon thereafter, I went to bed. I fell asleep for a short while, but suddenly I woke up, wide-eyed! The Holy Spirit gave me the words for the two stanzas John had pointed out that did not rhyme. I quickly found some paper and pen and wrote them down. The next day I studied what I had written. I deleted the original stanzas and typed the new ones. I showed the poem to John. He read it and said, "That's better."

I shared the poem with the school's secretary because I wanted the name of the script she had used for some school documents she had typed; I wanted to use this same script for the poem. After reading the poem, she offered to type the poem on parchment paper with the requested script. Of course, I was elated. Following is the poem the Holy Spirit downloaded to me.

A MOTHER'S POEM

In our family we have three girls
who are more precious than genuine pearls.
They each went to school to learn to be "cool"
so they would not go out into the world and be considered a fool.
So they grew, laughed, and sometimes cried.
They went to school and tried and tried.
The teachers thought they were very humble
because they did their work and did not grumble.
Then time passed, and they went away to college.
They worked hard and earned good grades for their dream cottage.
Two of the three are in the workforce today.
The third one is getting ready to enter the fray.
We know she, too, will be successful because she works hard but
also knows how to play.
Sometimes her life appears to be like a "soap,"
but we know that there is also hope.
Two of the three are now making their own money.
We know the third one, too, will soon earn her own money, and
eventually, we hope she will find her true honey.

Prior to writing this poem, my husband and I had said that our daughter's life was like a "soap opera" because she had two young men vying for her attention.

A NEW SCHOOL YEAR

A new school year had just begun, but I had one class that was proving to be rather difficult. In fact, there was a particular young man who made sure he kept me busy with his classroom antics. While sitting on the front row, he created many distractions, so I thought if I placed him in the back, he would not be such a distraction to the class. So, in this "backseat position," what do you think he did? Whenever I turned to write on the blackboard or whenever I turned my back on the class for whatever reason, he threw large wads of paper toward the front. He also resorted to using small pieces of paper for spit wades, which he used as missiles, shooting them through the air when I was not looking, of course. I became very frustrated because his antics were getting out of hand. One Friday, when the class was dismissed by the bell, I immediately got on the phone and called this student's home. I spoke to his dad and discussed his son's behavior. Unfortunately, I did not receive much parental support. Because of my stressful week, I developed a tension knot in my right shoulder area.

On Sunday Evangelist Larry was a guest speaker at the church. Toward the end of the service, he asked, "Would the person who is having a problem with their back come forth?" I should have immediately stepped forward, but I hesitated, so the evangelist specifically asked for the person who had a knot in their right shoulder to please come forward. I stepped forward. I had awakened that Sunday morning with severe pain in the right shoulder area, and the pain was so intense that it was hard for me to focus on anything. I stepped forward, and as I was standing next to him, Evangelist Larry quietly asked me the reason for my shoulder pain. With resignation in my voice, I replied, "School and stress." He then told me that I was not being very smart because I was trying to carry the load all by myself. He rebuked strife and oppression and declared that the joy of the Lord would be my strength. The next day, Monday morning, the pain and excruciating muscle knot was gone!

As a follow-up to this episode, this student graduated from high school and worked for a while at HEB in the fruit and vegetable section. One afternoon after a school day, I was in HEB shopping, and I saw him stacking vegetables. He acknowledged me; I chatted with him and reminded him of all the class trouble he created, including the spit wad episodes. He said, "Mrs. Panzarella, that was when I was in high school. I'm not like that anymore."

PRAYING FOR STUDENTS

The early morning hours are my prayer time. I read the Bible and pray for my family and for others who have prayer needs, for our nation, and for whatever is on my heart. At that time I also prayed for my students, perusing my seating charts. Not every day but some days, my eyes would pause on a student's name, and I would pray over the name. One morning, my eyes rested on a student's name on the chart who was in my Bible history class.

Then, I drove to school, parked the car, and began walking toward the school's front entrance. As I looked beyond the front door and into the entrance area, I saw the very student whose name my eyes had rested upon earlier that morning. She was standing near the front door. I had no idea, of course, why the Holy Spirit alerted me to pray for her. Because of this alert, I prayed for several weeks for this student and her family.

On another early morning time, as I was looking over my seating charts, my eyes rested on a boy's name in my English class. This young man was not applying himself. He was smart, but he was not working. I knew that he and his siblings lived with their grandmother. The student was not coming to tutorials and doing his make-up work even though I had reminded him several times. I telephoned the grandmother and told her about the situation. She assured me her grandson would be at the tutorial session. She was very emphatic and said to me, "He will be there!" While driving to school the next morning, I asked the Lord, "What should I say to this young man to motivate him to do his work?" I just kept talking to the Lord, asking, "What can I do? I know he is a capable student."

Heading toward my classroom, I walked up the stairs to my room on the second level. I spotted the young man. He was standing next to my door, waiting. I greeted him, unlocked the door, ushered him into the room, put away my things, and conversed some more under my breath to the Lord. Then, I turned and walked over to where the student had sat down. Looking directly at him, I said, "You look at me!" I was almost eyeball to eyeball. I repeated my words, "Look at me!" He slowly lifted his eyes and looked at me but *only* for a second. I said, "Your grandmother cares so much for you, and she wants you to be successful in school. If you do not do it for anybody else, do it for your grandmother!" He just sat there, looking at me. I repeated my words, "You do it for your grandmother!" Then I gave him the assignments. He finished the papers, handed them to me, and left. I would like to say there was a miraculous turnaround in his schoolwork, and he became a responsible student. However, that was not the case. I had to phone his grandmother two more times. He would come in, do his make-up work, and leave.

The following year, I was running an errand and checking with another English teacher on hallway A. This young man was standing by the door of his junior English class. I sensed his eyes following me as I walked along. I looked over at him; our eyes met for a moment. Within that quick eye contact, we exchanged a knowing and a remembrance of my words, "Do it for your grandmother!" At that moment, words were not needed.

Later, I had one more phone conversation with the student's grandmother. By this time, the young man was a first-year student at a private military school in England. During his freshman year at the school, he contracted a virus that quickly affected his nervous system. His roommate called 911 because the student's neck became locked in one position, and he could not move. Within forty-eight hours, the student died. I did not know anything about the virus attack nor what was transpiring, but during my prayer time, I felt a nudging by the Holy Spirit, and the thought came to me that I should call the grandmother. When I called, I told the grandmother I felt like I should call her. She quickly exclaimed that she was so glad I did. She told me about the virus, her grandson's sudden death, and the pending funeral plans. All I can say is the wonders of the Holy Spirit. Because of the alert by the Holy Spirit, I called and learned about the student's pending funeral. It was a very strange experience to stand by the casket of a student who had just been in your classroom a few years prior. Many of the boy's classmates were at the funeral dressed in their military uniforms. After the funeral service, these smartly-dressed, uniformed young men stood together in a cluster outside the church door; the anguish on their faces was apparent.

AN INTERVENTION

One weekend Sandra and I were returning from an Austin trip; the hour was very late. We were driving in the downtown area of quaint Needville, Texas. My gas gauge was getting very low. I kept watching it, but I thought to myself, *I will keep going, and surely I will find a gas station on down the road.* I stopped at a red light. There was a very dense fog that night. Out of this heavy fog, a police car appeared; it just seemed to come out of nowhere. The police officer asked me, "Where are you going?" I told him I was heading for a gas station.

He proceeded to tell me there were not any gas stations near me in the direction I was heading. He told me that I should turn around and go back to Rosharon, and he gave me directions to the gas station. At that time, I did not think much about this incident; I just followed the policeman's instructions, found the gas station, filled up the gas tank, and continued home. Later, when I analyzed the situation, it seemed almost surreal to me. The policeman's initial words were, "Where are you going?" and then he gave instructions on where to find a nearby gas station. If I had continued driving, I would have most likely run out of gas because there were no gas stations for many miles down the road.

SCHOOL OF PROPHESY

Mickey and Sandie Freed are pastors of Lifegate International Church, an apostolic/prophetic ministry and training center in Hurst, Texas, a suburb of Dallas. They have been in ministry for many years and are on Dr. Hamon's Christian International Ministry's board. As I previously stated, Dr. Hamon was the major participant in birthing the prophetic movement in the '50s. I have already mentioned that the Freeds have monthly first Friday night services, but periodically, they have a prophetic school in which they train and equip participants to flow in the Holy Spirit. Their Friday night services are excellent, and the worship is uplifting. Pastors Mickey and Sandie Freed have given some incredible teachings. Often, at the end of the service, attendees are instructed to turn to someone nearby, pray in the Spirit for a few minutes, flow in the Spirit, and then speak a prophetic word to the other person. It is amazing how the Holy Spirit shows up!

Several years ago, Sandra and I enrolled in their prophetic training program. We drove monthly to Bedford, Texas, which is near Dallas, for these Friday night services and attended the prophetic classes on Saturday morning. We were assigned numerous books to read, completed classroom assignments, wrote papers, participated in prophetic group activations, and gave prophetic words to others. When Sandra and I finished this training, we joined their monthly ministry teams for a while. There would be four or sometimes five prophetic teams ministering at the same time after the Friday evening service. The teams ministered to those who signed up for a prophetic word. There was always a team leader who oversaw a group of three to four people. These ministry times were always interesting. I particularly remember one Black family. My team and I walked down the row, ministering to each family member—the father, the mother, a sister, and the last person, a tall, lanky teenage brother. When the team came to the brother, it was my turn to prophesy. I remember the Holy Spirit telling this young man that he had on special tennis shoes, and no one would run faster after God than he. I remember him looking at me with a wide-eyed look as I spoke to him. During the evening service, I remember turning and looking around at the people in attendance, and for some reason, my eyes rested on this same tall, lanky young man. What was happening? The Holy Spirit was alerting me about this young man. And sure enough, this young man and his family were individuals assigned to our prophetic team, and the Holy Spirit ministered to the family.

At another prophetic session, I was placed on Vicky's team. Vicky prophesied to an individual, and then she turned and said to me, "Just pick whomever you wish." The only name I remembered from among those in attendance was a young lady named Danette. So I called Danette forward. I prayed for her and spoke a prophetic word to her. Then, another team member followed and gave the young girl additional prophetic words. While the other person was speaking to Danette, I received a strong impression. I saw Proverb 23:26 very clearly in my mind while the other person was prophesying to Danette. I kept repeating over and over to myself the words for Proverbs 23:26. When the other team member finished prophesizing, I told Danette that the Holy Spirit had a scripture for her. I quoted Proverbs 23:26 (AMP), which says, *"My son [or daughter], give me your heart and let your eyes delight in my ways."* I can only surmise the Holy Spirit was encouraging Danette to continue in her spiritual walk.

A PROPHETIC SERVICE PEARLAND, TEXAS

On July 15, 2000, Sandra, Dolores, and I attended a church service in Pearland, Texas. I had seen on TV an interview with a pastor who informed the TV audience about a prophetic meeting at his church in Pearland. The three of us decided to go. At this meeting, Sandra was given a prophetic word about her future husband. She had gone through a terrible divorce and was not sure she wanted to marry again. In fact, just that past week, Sandra had said to me, "I don't think I will marry again; I'm happy with my life as it is."

However, that evening a prophet from South Africa, a guest speaker, walked over to Sandra and asked her if she wanted to be married. She said, "I want to do what the Lord wants me to do." He persisted with his question and asked her again, "Do you want to be married?" Sandra paused and said, "Yes." He then replied to her, "God's got a man for you." He added that Sandra's future mate was going through a terrible trauma and instructed her to pray for him. What was the Lord doing? What was the purpose of all these questions? The Lord was using a prophetic word to "reset" Sandra's heart and to encourage her to pray for this man, her future husband, who was going through a terrible ordeal. Proverbs speaks about the importance of our words. Sandra had voiced her feelings about being single, stating, "I'm happy with my life right now," but the Lord had other plans for her. Because of this prophetic word, the Lord "reset" Sandra's heart, and she began praying for the healing mentioned in the prophetic word for her future husband, who was experiencing a trauma at that point in his life. It is amazing how the Lord encourages and directs us with prophetic words.

Later that same year, Sandra and I were praying in her home. While praying, the Holy Spirit gave me a strong impression about Sandra's future husband. In the spiritual realm, I saw him shaking hands with Patrick, Sandra's younger son. I also had the impression that

Sandra's future husband was tall, had lots of hair, and Patrick liked him. This, of course, encouraged Sandra.

Two years later, not realizing it at the time, John and I were used by the Lord as "matchmakers." We introduced Sandra to Jim, her future husband. And guess what—Sandra's husband-to-be was tall, had lots of hair, and Patrick liked him. When Jim was courting Sandra, he was a frequent guest in our home. Jim had been a longtime friend of John's, and he was now a widower. Also, John and Jim had many similarities. They were both engineers and loved to grow various plants and citrus trees.

As an added note to this episode, there was a knock on our front door one day. I opened the door to a florist delivery person. The delivery person stood at the door, holding a bouquet of flowers. I said, "You must have the wrong address." I thought to myself, *Who would be sending me flowers?* The delivery person double-checked the address and said, "No, I have the correct address." Somehow, during all the years John and I have been married, he has not acquired the etiquette of sending flowers to me. The mystery was solved; Sandra's future husband sent me flowers in appreciation for being a guest in our home.

A DECISION

When I retired from teaching, I was not sure if I had made the right decision because I thought perhaps I had gotten out of step with the Lord's timing. I kept going back and forth in my mind about my decision, so during those summer months, I made an appointment to speak with the principal about substituting. At our morning meeting, he told me, of course, that he could not predict what would happen in the fall, but he would keep me in mind if something did occur. By the end of the first six weeks of school, a ninth-grade English teacher had submitted a pregnancy leave of absence, and the principal called me. The classes were a real challenge. I had some very trying days because this teacher did not have very good control of her classes.

The following school year, I informed the principal that I would be available to substitute if anything came up. A week before school began, I had a very vivid dream. At that time, we were visiting our middle daughter and her family in Plano, Texas. In this detailed dream, I was at a celebration. There was a party, and a cake was on the table, but it was clear to me in the dream that this was not a birthday cake, but a cake was present because of a celebration. The cake was decorated with a very bold handwriting on top of it. In this dream the ladies in the English department, whom I had worked with for many years, were all sitting together at a circular table, and for some reason, they were clapping for me.

Because we were visiting and not at home, I scrambled to find a piece of paper to write down the dream. I have learned from experience that if I do not immediately write down a dream upon awakening, it "slips" away, and later I do not remember the details and sometimes even the dream. The dream occurred on a Sunday. This was the day we were leaving for home.

The next day, Monday, the high school principal called and told me an English position had occurred. In this instance, an assistant principal at our high school had accepted a position as a principal in Houston, which left a vacancy for her position. An English teacher, whom I had worked with, had just finished her administrative degree. She was promoted to this vacated assistant principal's position. Because of the shifting of personnel, an opening had occurred in the English department, and the principal called me. This happened right before school started.

School districts always have teacher in-service the week prior to beginning classes. On the first day of in-service, our principal always introduced the new or returning teachers. I was a returning teacher. My dream materialized before my eyes. The English teachers were all sitting together at a round table to my left, just like in my dream. The principal called my name, and I stood up. The English teachers immediately clapped their hands when the principal called my name. Afterward Sandra, my friend, turned and said to me, "They all clapped for you!"

Sometimes the Lord allows time to pass before fully understanding a dream or a prophetic word, and much, much later in the school year, the total understanding of this dream came to me. I had not pondered too much about the bold handwriting on top of the cake that I had seen in my dream because I was so busy with my classes. However, as the semester progressed, I was walking to the office one day, and the Holy Spirit brought the details of the dream to my remembrance: the decorated cake, the bold handwriting, and the teachers at the table. At that very moment, the realization hit me! The bold handwriting on top of the cake was the principal's handwriting! I had never made the connection! One can only marvel at the Holy Spirit.

THE UNEXPECTED

Around 2006, Evangelist Dick ministered at our church. During the Sunday morning service, our pastor began calling on individuals to be ministered to prophetically. After listening for a few minutes, I said to myself, *This is a big church; I do not have to worry about being called on.* I proceeded to open my notebook to take notes. *The very next minute,* and *much to my surprise*, the pastor called my name! Pastor Dick did not know that at that time in my life, I was experiencing anguish in my soul because of some words spoken to me. In fact, I was even having trouble sleeping. I did not share my feelings with anyone, but the Lord knew, and He wanted to bring peace to my heart. I typed out the prophetic words spoken to me, studied them, and prayed over them. Peace did return to my heart as I read and reread the prophetic words spoken to me on that day.

A HOLY SPIRIT CONNECTION

In 2006, the church organized military gift boxes to send to American soldiers overseas. A group of ladies met to fill boxes with items for shipment to soldiers. After finishing our task, one of the ladies mentioned to several of us that her son was in the military, and she said her son was on suicide watch and, of course, she was concerned about him. Upon hearing this, the lady in charge of our project asked several of us to pray for the mother. She then turned to me and asked me to pray for the mother and her son. Diane was standing near my right shoulder, and another lady was to my left. When I began praying, both ladies simultaneously placed their hands on my shoulders. Immediately, a warm feeling permeated both shoulders. In fact, that warm sensation remained on my shoulders for about fifteen minutes or so.

On Sunday I shared this unusual experience with the pastor. He immediately responded and said, "That was a prayer of agreement." Matthew 18:19 (AMPC) says, "*Again I tell you, if two of you on earth agree (harmonize together, make a symphony together) about whatever [anything and everything] they may ask, it will come to pass and be done for them by My Father in heaven.*" The two ladies and I were in total agreement (harmony) in our hearts concerning this mom's son. Because of the power of agreement, we were assured that this young soldier would be safe from any suicidal attempts.

THE HOLY SPIRIT ON THE MOVE

In 2007, our church began inviting life speaker/life coach/Pastor Tim to minister at our church. During his visits, he would preach, but at the end of his message, he often called individuals to the front to minister to them or give them a prophetic word. At a Sunday evening service, I was sitting in the center area, which was about midway in the church's pews. Pastor Tim was speaking to the audience, but while speaking, he kept looking at me as he spoke to the congregation. Even though there was some distance between where he was standing and where I was sitting, his eyes remained focused on me. He continued talking for a minute or two more, and when he finished his point, he turned and said, "Would the lady in the jacket with flowers on it come up here?" I was the lady in the jacket with flowers! I walked to the front, and when I was about three feet or so from him, he looked directly at me and said, "The Lord is going to give you some more!" Then, suddenly, something that felt like electricity went through my body—head to toe. It almost caused me to lose my balance, but I caught myself. Later, I thought to myself, *Why had I been called to the front?* Reflecting on the matter, I realized that the Lord was strengthening me in my walk with Him.

A NEW YEAR'S EVE CELEBRATION

In 2007, when Sandra and Jim, our good friends, were dating, I noticed on Terry MacAlmon's website that he would be the featured praise and worship leader for a New Year's Eve service at a church in Plano, Texas. I told Sandra about the event, and she and Jim joined John and me. There were about 1,000 people at the service. During the worship service, Terry MacAlmon shared about a worship time in South Africa. He had been invited by a church to lead praise and worship service for the Lord; he was in a large auditorium filled to capacity. He shared with us that people were standing outside the auditorium watching the performance. Terry MacAlmon told the audience that he felt sad seeing all those people who could not join others because of the fire code, which prevented more people in the building. He also shared with us about an unusual experience that night in South Africa. He said that at one point during the worship service, the people spontaneously began singing in what he described as "waves of songs and worship." One group began a song, and then the other group responded, and then the second group sang a song, and the first group responded. He said you would have thought it had been rehearsed because it was so synchronized. He added that in this atmosphere of worship, people began to be healed. As Terry MacAlmon was describing this South African spontaneous worship and healing service, a man sitting at the end of our row, to the right of Sandra, Jim, John, and myself, began jumping up and down and yelping. You would have thought a thousand ants were biting him; the man just kept jumping up and down and yelping. What the audience did not realize was that the Holy Spirit was working and healing this man during this worship time. The explanation came forth during the midnight communion.

Midnight arrived at this New Year's Eve service, and we took communion as the pastor led everyone in prayer. After communion the pastor said, "I'm not going to embarrass this man," indicating in the direction of the man who had jumped up and down, but then the pastor changed his mind and said, "Yes, I am." He then asked the man to stand up. The pastor proceeded to tell the audience, "You have no idea what this man has been through nor how long we have been praying for him." What had happened? The Holy Spirit had touched this man exactly at the same moment that Terry MacAlmon related to the audience about the healings that had taken place during the praise and worship service in South Africa. We were never told the man's problems, but it is remarkable that the Holy Spirit showed up in a timely fashion—just as Terry MacAlmon was discussing about this unique healing service.

When I returned home, I related this experience to my pastor. He immediately responded with, "The Lord goes after the *one*." So, no matter what we are experiencing, the Lord knows our circumstances, and He is concerned about every individual. That should be an encouragement to us all!

THE 2008 STOCK MARKET CRASH

In 2008, the United States experienced a stark drop in the financial markets. The stock market plunged downward quite dramatically. Investments plummeted in value, and other markets were affected because of the stock market's decline. About that time, John and I were visiting Sandra and Jim, who were now married and living in the Valley. Organizing for the trip, I decided to bring a Bible I had on my bookshelf. This Bible had specific scriptures set off within shaded gray box areas, accompanied with commentary. We were busy doing things with Jim and Sandra, going here and there, but at one point, I said to myself, *I have a few free minutes, so I will sit down and read the Bible.* I began reading in Jeremiah. I noticed that Jeremiah 17:7–8 was set off in one of those gray boxes.

Jeremiah 17:7–8 (AMPC) says, "*For he shall be like a tree planted by the waters that spreads out its roots by the river; and it shall not see and fear when heat comes; but its leaf shall be green. It shall not be anxious and full of care in the year of drought, nor shall it cease yielding fruit.*"

This scripture caught my attention. I kept pondering and thinking about it. I decided to memorize it. John and I returned home. On Sunday, I went to the church's 7:00 a.m. prayer service. The pastor prayed for the service, the church's various ministries, and then others also prayed. When I prayed, I prayed Jeremiah 17:8, the scripture that had recently caught my attention. As I was returning to my seat, the pastor asked me to repeat the scripture address that I had just prayed. At the eleven o'clock service, much to my surprise, the pastor read Jeremiah 17:7–8 to the congregation. What can we surmise? The Holy Spirit used Jeremiah 17:7–8 to reassure the congregation that everything would eventually work out concerning the financial and economic situation America was experiencing in 2008.

The Holy Spirit even reassured the congregation a second time. As we were being dismissed after a Wednesday evening service, Isaiah 58:11 came to my mind. I told my husband to wait a minute because I wanted to speak to the pastor. I went to the podium and told the pastor I had a scripture for him. I shared Isaiah 58:11 (AMPC), which says, *"And the Lord shall guide you continually and satisfy you in drought and in dry places...And you shall be like a watered garden and like a spring of water whose waters fail not."*

The following Sunday the pastor read Isaiah 58:11 to the congregation; he commented that Isaiah 58:11 was similar to Jeremiah 17:7–8. Again, the Holy Spirit was underscoring the fact that we should have peace in our hearts, rest in the Lord, and trust Him amid the 2008 financial upheaval.

NOON PRAYER - PART 1

At one of our church's noon prayer sessions, I requested prayer for my middle daughter. She holds a mid-management position for a computer company in Plano, Texas. At that time, her company had been bought out and acquired by an out-of-state company. On that Tuesday evening, our daughter called and informed John and me about the acquisition of her company by an out-of-state company. She was concerned about the situation and commented to us that she might not have a job by the end of the week. She said that the new boss had decided to essentially fire all employees of the old company (my daughter's company).

The next day, we had our Wednesday noon prayer session; I related the dire situation concerning my daughter and the other employees. At this prayer session, we prayed for my daughter's job and the other employee's jobs, plus we prayed for the new boss to assess the situation more fairly. That was Wednesday. Friday evening our daughter called to tell us about a surprising turn of events. She informed us that one of the new company managers walked into the head boss' office and said to him, "Do you realize what you are doing? Do you realize the impact this action will have on the whole company and our inability to function?" The results: The boss rescinded his decision. My daughter and the other employees retained their positions, and the former employees were merged into the new company. The Lord heard our prayers and moved quickly by that Friday!

NOON PRAYER - PART 2

At another noon prayer session, Pastor Robert led the prayer meeting. At the beginning of the service, Pastor Robert was feeling rather pensive and said, "Does God really speak to us?" I quickly responded, "Yes, He does!" I added, "I just read Job 33:14–15 during my morning prayer time, and Job 33:14–15

(NIV) says, '*For God does speak—now one way, now another—though no one perceives it. In a dream, in a vision of the night, when deep sleep falls on people as they slumber in their beds.'"*

Pastor Robert stopped, thought a minute, turned, and silently read Job 33:14–15. He then proceeded to read Job 33:14–15 out loud to everyone. That evening Pastor Robert was the pastor to lead the Wednesday evening service. He began his opening message by reading Job 33:14–15 to the congregation. Isn't it amazing how the Holy Spirit works!

A LUNCH EVENT - PART 1

One day, the Holy Spirit "showed up" at school and helped me! Sandra and I usually brought our lunches to school and visited and chatted at lunchtime. On one such occasion, I was visiting with Sandra in her room, sitting in a student's desk, eating part of my lunch, which was a raw carrot. However, when I swallowed the carrot, pieces became stuck in my esophagus. Those little pieces of carrots lodged in my throat. The pain was so severe that I had to lay my head on the desk. Sandra asked me if I wanted her to call the school nurse. I told her I would just try to wait a few minutes to see if the pain subsided. After a while, the pain became intolerable. I walked over to Sandra's trash receptacle, and I said, "Oh, Lord, in the name of Jesus, please help me!" Instantly, I felt air bubbles move upward from my stomach area into my esophagus. Those air bubbles then pushed the stuck carrots up into my mouth! Yuck! I immediately spit them out into the trash can. Then, I felt fine! I was so grateful to be relieved of the excruciating pain, and my next class was scheduled to start soon. I was elated; now I felt normal! I could finish the school day pain-free! First Kings 8:28 (NIV) says the "...*Lord my God. Hear the cry and the prayer that your servant is praying in your presence this day.*" The Lord certainly heard my prayer for help.

A LUNCH EVENT - PART 2

There was another interesting lunch incident. This time Sandra joined me for lunch in my room; we were visiting and just beginning our lunches when I turned to speak to Sandra, and in the spiritual realm, I saw a big spider hanging just above her head. I said, "Sandra, I see a large spider above your head!" I added, "The spider is just sitting there; there isn't a cobweb or anything." We discussed the spiritual implications of spiders. I mentioned to Sandra that the spider might be related to the incident in the hall that week where a student had said some ugly words to her. This student had a history of rude behavior, and even the assistant principal was aware of this young man's outbursts.

That evening, Sandra and I attended Wednesday evening church. Linda, who now works for Aglow International in Washington State, walked into the church's sanctuary and spotted Sandra. She walked straight over to her and waved her hands wildly above Sandra's head. Then, Linda told Sandra that when she had walked into the sanctuary, she had seen a large spider above her head. This was the same spider I had seen at lunch. We immediately prayed protection over Sandra, rebuking any negative words or any intentions against her.

A PRAYER SERVICE

One early Sunday morning, as I drove to our church's 7:00 a.m. prayer service, I received a spiritual impression. I saw a group of men standing in unity in a semicircle. At the end of our prayer service, I turned to leave. I glanced back for a moment, and to my surprise, the pastor and the other men were all standing together in a semicircle just like I had seen in the spirit realm while driving to church. I shared with them my impression, and I said to them, "I feel the Lord wants me to pray for all of you because you represent godly models for the men of the church to follow." I prayed Proverbs 2:20 (AMPC) for all the men of the church to "*...walk in the way of good men, and keep to the paths of the [consistently] righteous (the upright, in right standing with God).*"

A WORD FOR THE PASTOR

There was another 7:00 a.m. morning prayer service that was memorable. While driving, I prayed in the spirit. Suddenly, the Holy Spirit just dropped into my spirit the word *transmitter*. In the spiritual realm, I could almost see the word *transmitter* hovering just above my eyes, and then I felt the word *transmitter* drop into my spirit! It was certainly an unusual experience. I just kept repeating the word *transmitter* over and over to myself as I drove along, and I kept asking the Holy Spirit, "What does that mean?"

Arriving at the church, I sat down and joined everyone for the prayer service. A few minutes later, the pastor entered the sanctuary by the side door. As the pastor walked to join us, I silently laughed to myself because the shirt the pastor was wearing had the symmetry of hundreds of circles, which looked like little "radars." I immediately knew that the "radars" on his shirt were symbols of transmitters! At that very moment, I realized that the pastor was wearing his *transmitter* shirt!

After the pastor prayed for the Sunday service, we gathered around him and prayed for the pending service. I shared with everyone the experience I had while driving to church. Then, I prayed for our pastor, God's transmitter of biblical principles. I also prayed the pastor would be the "the connector, the transmitter" of God's Word to the people. After the prayer session ended, I shared more details with our pastor about the word *transmitter* and what had transpired as I drove to the church. I commented to him that his shirt was a symbol of "God's radar signals," which would be emitted to the people.

The pastor then shared that he had been indecisive that morning about which shirt to wear, and for a few minutes, he could not make up his mind. Then, he chose the shirt he was wearing, his *transmitter* shirt. I can only surmise that the word *transmitter* dropped into my spirit the moment the pastor decided to wear his *transmitter* shirt, and I can also surmise that the Holy Spirit used his *transmitter* shirt to speak an encouragement to him!

WARNING DREAMS

We all have dreams, whether we remember them or not. Dream books classify and categorize the various types of dreams. One type of dream is a warning dream. I have had several warning dreams, which are shared below.

Dream #1: On July 28, 2009, I had a dream that I was standing in front of my house, and a long, black car with low side windows pulled up alongside our curb and stopped in front of our house. In this vivid dream, I took a few steps forward to see if I could see the driver, but I could not see into the car very well. I did sense that there was someone else in the car besides the driver. I just knew in my heart, however, that it was not John, my husband. If you read books on dreams and their symbols, the front yard represents an event in the future.

At first, I did not have a clear understanding of this dream. At that time, John's mother, Louise Panzarella, was ninety-four years old. Even though she was ninety-four, she had such a dynamic personality that the family never thought of her as being old. It never occurred to me that this dream pertained to Louise. Our family just thought she would live for many years. This dream occurred five months before Louise passed away. Months later, I realized this was a warning dream concerning Louise. Later, I also realized that the long black car in the dream was a hearse!

Dream #2: On December 18, 2009, I had a dream that my father, who had passed away several years before, was sitting at a large banquet table with Louise, John's mother. Louise was still with us; however, the Holy Spirit was alerting me that Louise's passing on earth was imminent. I told John about my dream. He commented to me, "Don't have any more dreams like that." Nine days later, Louise passed away!

Dream #3: On July 7, 2011, I had a dream about my friend Sandra. In this particular dream, I was standing on the sidewalk in our front yard, looking at the front of our house. Then, I turned to the right; I saw an ambulance coming down our street, rushing at top speed with lights flashing. A police car traveling at a top speed also followed the ambulance. Then, both vehicles cut across our front lawn and made an abrupt ninety-degree turn into our house, disappearing into the window of our study. I stood on the sidewalk, observing all this action. Then, the dream shifted. Next, I was chatting with Sandra on my cell phone, but I kept telling her that I could not hear her very well because my phone battery was weak.

The Manifestation of Dream #3

A year later, Sandra, her husband, Jim, and her oldest son were traveling on I-20 early one morning, heading to Fort Worth for a doctor's appointment during the a.m. rush hour. A large, oversized truck did not see their car, and the truck driver moved into their lane, causing their car to slide down a steep embankment. Jim and Sandra's son was bruised and shaken, but Sandra was the one who was injured. She had a broken back! Several days later, back surgery ensued with the doctor placing four sets of bolts and screws along her spine, eight total, to strengthen and support the breakage in her spine.

An Understanding of Dream #3

When I had dream #3, I certainly did not understand its meaning, but I continued to pray about it over time. Several months after the accident, the Holy Spirit gave me revelation about the dream. I also realized the fact that if I had not prayed, the outcome of the car accident could possibly have been much worse. I also understood why the ambulance and police car were rushing so fast; Sandra and her family were involved in a terrible accident.

Dream #4: On February 20, 2013, I had another warning dream, but this time it concerned our church. This dream occurred at three different time intervals during the night. Each time I was given part of the dream, and each time I made myself get up and write down the details. Then, I made a dream chart so I could analyze and decipher more clearly the meaning of the dream.

Following is an analysis and chart describing dream #4.

THE DREAM

Title of dream: A Man at Church
Date: February 20, 2013
Setting: Outside grounds near the church's office

Description of the Dream

_12:10 a.m._–I am not a late-night person. I had been asleep for a while. I woke up from this dream and felt an urgency to write everything down. In this particular dream, I saw a man walking on the south side of the church's building; the south side is where the church's office is located. The man had a gun in his hand.

_2:30 a.m._–I awoke again at 2:30 a.m. In this short sequel, I saw numerous vultures flying in a circular formation in the sky, circling over the church's adjacent property.

5:30 a.m.—I had a strong impression in my spirit, and I sensed the question, "Why is this perpetrator on the land?" I kept repeating the word *perpetrator* to myself as I walked to get a pad and pen.

The Dream Chart

Symbol	*Interpretation of the Dream*
Man was walking with a gun on the sidewalk.	Guns can represent accusations, slander, gossip, criticism, or even words released by someone with hurtful intentions.
Vultures were circling the church's property.	Vultures are scavenger birds and demonic in nature. They can represent a murmuring and complaining spirit. They are extremely negative in nature, unclean and impure as an evil person.
In my spirit, I sensed the question, "Why is the perpetrator on the land?"	Definition of *perpetrator*: a culprit, one accused of or charged with a crime.

I prayed over this dream, and then I emailed the dream and the chart to my pastor. At that time, I did not know anything about the circumstances that were occurring at the church. Responding to the email, the pastor called me. He informed me that the man who had been under contract to cut the church's grass was not doing a very good job, so the man was told his services were no longer needed. Next, the pastor began receiving several threatening phone calls from this man to the point that the pastor hired a police officer for the church's Sunday service. At that time, having a police officer on duty at a church was not an everyday occurrence, and, of course, everyone was surprised to see a police officer at church. Nowadays, because of violence at many churches, no one is surprised to see police officers at church services, but in early 2013, this was not the case.

AN ALERT TO PRAY

Several years ago, there was a family who had attended our church for many years. At one point, the doctors informed the parents that their daughter, who was in high school at the time, had leukemia. The daughter endured all kinds of medical procedures and tests at MD Anderson, and eventually, after many treatments, the leukemia was arrested. The daughter graduated from high school, attended college, met her husband-to-be, and married him. Several years later, much to the couple's dismay, the leukemia returned. The young couple decided to move back to Lake Jackson to be near Houston and the doctors at MD Anderson. Again, the young lady underwent tests, procedures, and medications, and a plan of action was initiated; it was a long process. The doctors finally reached a point where they told the young couple and the parents that they had done all they could do. The young lady remained in the hospital very sick. The doctors began ministering medications to relieve the excruciating pain. Finally, the situation became so dire, bleak, and painful for the daughter that she reached the decision herself to abstain from taking any more medication. Thus, she began the dying process. The family, of course, was by her side at the hospital.

At that time, John and I were visiting our middle daughter in Plano, Texas. I did not know anything about the situation or the daughter's grave medical condition. However, the day the daughter made the decision to stop taking *all* medications, I was awakened at 3:15 a.m. that morning. I sensed an urgency to pray about something or someone. Since we were not home, there was not any place where I thought I could sit down and pray, so I went into the upstairs bathroom. I prayed in the spirit for a while because of the urgent feeling I had. The next morning, around 11:00 a.m., the pastor's wife texted me that the daughter had passed away, and she related to me the details about the daughter's decision. A few minutes later, the realization came to me why I was awakened at 3:15 a.m. This was the exact time the daughter had passed away! When I was praying at 3:15 a.m., I sensed the Lord was extending empathy to someone or to a situation. I later realized that the compassion and empathy I sensed were not only for the daughter but for the parents. In fact, at the time I was praying, I felt the Lord was extending peace and comfort to someone. Later, I realized that "someone" was the parents.

I told Dolores, my friend, the details about the 3:15 a.m. episode. Several weeks later at the end of a Wednesday evening service, Dolores spotted the mom. She walked the mom over to me and asked me to repeat to the mom what had happened the night I was awakened to pray. I told the mother all the details—3:15 a.m. time, the strong urgency to pray, and the text the next morning about the daughter's death. I also related to the mom that I sensed during my prayer time that the Lord wanted to especially bring comfort and peace to someone or a situation. Later, of course, I realized that feeling of comfort was for the family. Hearing this, the mother, of course, was comforted and encouraged.

I hope sharing these dreams will encourage others to write down their dreams and pray over them.

THE HOLY SPIRIT AND TWO YOUNG MEN

In 2016, we visited our youngest daughter in Austin, Texas, and I attended Arise Ministries' Friday night worship and prophetic service. During their praise and worship time, I turned and looked around at the individuals in attendance. While gazing around, two young men caught my attention. These two young men had a radiance or what I would describe as an aura surrounding them. Later during the service, these two men were the very ones who were singled out by the church's prophetic team to receive a prophetic word. As I sat there, I kept thinking about the aura and what I had seen. This puzzled me.

A few minutes later, Pastor Vance walked over to me and prophesied the following:

> "Rosamond, you are very—you are—well, you're kinda like my granddaughter. She observes. And you are an observer, but you are trying to figure out exactly what you are observing. And the Spirit of God says, 'I'm exposing to you, and I'm showing you the heavenlies.'"

Isn't this amazing? The Lord singled me out to explain to me via a prophetic word the special aura I had seen on those two young men. That is remarkable! This aura was a heavenly sign indicating that these two men would receive a prophetic word. Have you ever wondered how a person flowing in the prophetic knows when to give words to a specific individual? Now we know. You just look for the *aura, the radiance* created by the Holy Spirit.

A REPEAT OF GENESIS 18:14

Two years later, on October 6, 2018, I again attended Arise Ministries' Friday night worship service. During this evening service, Pastor Vance approached me and said, "Let me see your hand." He said that I had hands for healing. Holding my hand, he then called a lady over to me. He placed my hand in her hand and instructed me to pray for her because she was a diabetic. I prayed for the lady. Then, Pastor Vance called over Josie, a member of his staff, to stand in the gap in prayer for her sister, who had non-Hoskins lymphoma and leukemia. He asked me to pray for Josie's sister. While praying for the sister, I concluded the prayer with Genesis 18:14 (NIV), which says, "*Is anything too hard for the LORD?*"

Five months later, on March 1, 2019, we returned to Austin for another visit with our daughter. I again attended Arise Ministries' Friday night worship service. After worship and prayer, some members of the church stood in front of the congregation, giving prophetic words to individuals. At that time, I was concerned about a stressful situation in my family. One of the ministering ladies walked over to me and spoke a prophetic word to me, and her last words to me were, "The Lord wishes to bring solace to you about a family situation."

What was so remarkable about this word is that when the lady finished speaking to me, a man in the congregation concluded this prophetic word with a special message to me. The man said to me and those in attendance, "The Lord has been reminding me of the scripture Genesis 18:14, which was the scripture you spoke over Josie the last time you were here." He then proceeded to read Genesis 18:14 (NIV), saying, "*Is anything too hard for the Lord?*" Then, he said to me, "I feel the Lord is speaking that scripture to you tonight."

Isn't that remarkable? The Lord used the same scripture, Genesis 18:14, that I had spoken *five months prior* while praying for the healing of Josie's sister, but this time the Holy Spirit used Genesis 18:14 to convey a message to me about my family and a stressful situation.

A SURPRISE MEETING

I listen to *Point of View* radio on my iPhone quite frequently in the mornings. Every Friday, the host and moderator have guests who discuss an overview of the previous week's news, events, court cases, or political situations in our nation. Kelly Shackelford, president/CEO and chief counsel of First Liberty, a premiere legal organization that defends religious liberty in the state of Texas and throughout the US, is often a guest on *Point of View*. Kelly Shackelford often gives candid judicial assessments concerning legal cases First Liberty is handling. During one of the radio programs, the moderator of *Point of View* informed its listeners that Kelly Shackelford would be a guest at Texas Values' Faith, Family, and Freedom Gala in Houston, Texas. At the same time, I also received an email from Texas Values about the event. The email mentioned that Kelly Shackleford and Texas' attorney general would be speakers. I told John that I thought it would be an interesting event to attend. I responded to the email, and we made plans to attend.

On the day of the event, we drove in the five o'clock Houston traffic, found a parking spot near the Hilton Hotel, and signed in with the check-in lady for our dinner table assignment. The lady assigned us to dinner table number three. When the dining area opened, John and I walked around and located table number three, which to my surprise, was near the speaker's podium. I thought, *This is great! We're close to the front and can see the speakers very well.* Table number three already had some individuals standing by it. We spoke with the man to our left. He told us that he and his wife had been friends with Kelly Shackleford for a long time. Then, as we turned around, the Texas attorney general's wife, who is now a Texas state senator, turned and saw us and introduced herself to us. I could only see the back of a man standing near us, and people were crowding around, talking to him. Then, this man, the attorney general of Texas, turned, saw us, shook our hands, and introduced himself. Without even thinking, words just tumbled out of my mouth. I said that he did not have to introduce himself because I prayed for him every day. I added, in fact, that I prayed for all three of Texas' leaders—the governor, the lieutenant governor, and himself, the attorney general. He said that he liked to attend events like this to hear that people were praying. He said he was appreciative of the prayers and added, "This is a spiritual battle."

After this brief conversation, his attention was diverted because other people were wanting to talk to him. While

I was speaking with Texas' attorney general, John quickly assessed the situation and realized that we were probably assigned to the wrong table. He then left to double-check our table number. I did not dare leave my spot because there were so many people at the event that John would have trouble finding me in the crowd. While waiting, I again talked with the man at table number three and mentioned to him that we were not sure about our table assignment. He was gracious and did a quick calculation and said there were eight places at the table, and they just might have to put Kelly Shackleford somewhere else. He nodded toward his daughter and her husband and an accompanying friend who had just appeared at the table. His daughter, looking puzzled, said she was not sure if they were supposed to be at table number three or table number four. I had no idea at that moment that John and I were the reason for the confusion. Right after that, John returned. We were at the wrong table! The check-in lady said we should be at table number thirty-eight!

Before leaving, I spotted Kelly Shackleford, who was standing nearby. I introduced myself to him and told him that I listened to him on Point of View's Friday Weekend Edition, and the fact that he was one of the speakers at the event was one of the reasons we decided to come.

**A quick conversation with Kelly Shackleford,
CEO, chief counsel, and president of First Liberty.**

Then, I quickly caught up with John, following him to table number thirty-eight. We went from table number three, which was located at the front of the room, to table number thirty-eight, which was located at the back of the room. As we walked to table number thirty-eight, I double-checked with John to see if I had correctly heard the check-in lady's initial assignment for us—table number three. John said, "Yes, I also heard the same thing, table number three." As we sat down at our new location, John commented that we might be sitting near the waiter's station. He looked around and then added, "I wouldn't be surprised if they ask us to wash the dishes!"

Prior to this gala event, I had saved several newspaper articles about the Texas attorney general and his prior business associates who had brought lawsuits against him, which, of course, made the newspaper's headline. I had saved the articles and prayed for the attorney general and the situation. You might say to yourself that this was just a coincidence; however, Proverbs 16:33 (AMPC) says, *The lot is cast into the lap, but the decision is wholly of the Lord [even the events that seem accidental are really ordered by Him].*" I felt I had received a "wink" from the Lord because I had been praying for this man.

VALUES VOTER SUMMIT
WASHINGTON, DC - SEPTEMBER 2016

More Surprises

I listen frequently to the *Washington Watch* radio program on my iPhone. On one of the broadcasts, the president of Family Research Council mentioned Family

Research Council's planned event, Values Voter Summit in Washington, DC. I also received a Family Research Council email about the pending event. I mentioned to John that I would like to go. He commented that he did not think we would meet people like we had at the Texas Values event in Houston. I told him you never know whom you might meet. We bought our plane tickets, made hotel arrangements, and attended the all-day Friday and Saturday affair. We also attended the Saturday night gala dinner, which had a special speaker.

The year 2016 was an election year, which made everything more interesting. Upon our arrival at the hotel, we were informed that Donald Trump and Mike Pence would be the first two speakers on the schedule for Friday—the next day. The next morning, we stood in a lengthy line, went through the Secret Service security check, and walked into the meeting area. As scheduled, Donald Trump was the first speaker on the agenda. Then Mike Pence, the vice-presidential nominee, followed presidential nominee Trump. However, before Mike Pence spoke, there was a lunch interval. We were reminded that if anyone chose to leave the room and eat at another location and return, then they would have to go through another security check to reenter to hear Mike Pence speak. Most everyone chose to stay in the large room and order off the hotel's quick menu of sandwiches or salad. Immediately after the lunch break, the vice-presidential nominee Pence spoke.

The speaker who followed Mike Pence was Dr. James Dobson. Speaking to the audience, Dr. Dobson related the 2016 voting choices to his recent eye exam. Dr. Dobson said, "Is it number one or number two?" During that pre-election time, no one was quite sure about presidential nominee Donald Trump and his presidency. The public only had Trump's words, his proposals, and his list of potential Supreme Court nominees as criteria for his presidency.

Along with the speakers, numerous media networks were present with all their equipment, wires, cameras, and, of course, the journalists. They were set up in the back of the room. The gala dinner event took place Saturday night. On Sunday morning Family Research Council held a Sunday morning worship service at the hotel. Our flight did not leave until later in the day, so we attended the service. During praise and worship, John, pointing to my left, leaned over to me and said to me, "I think that is Dr. Dobson over there." I looked over to where he indicated, but I could only see the back of a very tall man's head. I was not sure if that was Dr. Dobson or not. However, when Dr. Dobson's wife, Shirley, joined him, I knew John was right. After the Sunday morning service, many people left, but a few stayed, mingling and talking with Dr. Dobson and his wife, Shirley.

Dr. Dodson was engaged in a conversation with a man. I introduced myself to his wife, Shirley Dodson.

**Shirley Dodson was so gracious
as I related my classroom story to her.**

I told her I wanted to share with her a story relating to Dr. Dobson's radio program. I informed her that

I taught English at a high school, and every morning while getting ready for school, I always listened to Dr. Dobson's radio program. However, one day the radio station changed its schedule and did not air Dr. Dobson's radio program. This was the only free time I had to listen to Dr. Dobson. To remedy the situation, I carried a radio to my first-period class, placed the radio on the floor directly behind my desk, and recorded Dr. Dobson's program on another station at 8:30 a.m. I did this every day. So, while teaching and conducting class, I would just matter-of-factly walk over at 8:30 a.m., push the lever, record Dr. Dobson's program, and continue talking to the class. At the end of the school day, I would then take the recording home and listen to Dr. Dobson's program the next morning while getting ready for school. This was my regular routine.

However, on a busy school day, I had an early morning parent conference in the counselor's office, and the meeting went overtime. I was not able to return to my first period when class began. Somehow the office had overlooked the fact that I needed a substitute; no one was sent to oversee my class. As a result, my class had some "free" time. At 8:30 a.m., one of the girls in the class promptly walked over to the radio behind my desk and pushed the lever to begin recording Dr. Dobson's program. As an added note, I had one boy who thought he might have a free "wandering day" that day. However, just as I was coming up the flight of stairs heading to the classroom, I intercepted him and stopped any nomadic intentions he might have entertained.

When I finished my story, Shirley Dodson commented, "I will be sure to tell him." As we were finishing our conversation, Dr. Dodson turned and joined us.

Dr. Dobson explained to me how Family Research Council was established.

Dr. Dobson began discussing the fact that Family Research Council had been established in the 1980s for the purpose of representing families and family-related issues in Congress. He went on to say that years ago, he telephoned the current president of Family Research Council, asking him to take over as president of Family Research Council because the leadership was stepping down to pursue other interests.

Later, traveling on the DC subway, heading back to the airport for our flight, I turned to John and said, "Now, what was that you said to me about not meeting interesting people at this event?"

VALUES VOTER SUMMIT
WASHINGTON, DC - SEPTEMBER 2017

The FBI at Work

We returned to Washington, DC, to attend Family Research Council's 2017 Values Voter Summit. President Trump had promised Family Research Council that if he won the 2016 election, he would return to speak in 2017.

So early Friday morning, everyone went through an extensive security check because President Trump was the first scheduled speaker. The next day, Saturday, everyone went through another security check. At this meeting, Vice President Pence was scheduled to be the first speaker of the day. Entering the large seating area, John suggested that we sit on the front row but on the left side, so we found some seats and settled in.

While sitting there, several Secret Service agents appeared, walking right by us, checking things out. It was interesting to watch them at work. Next, a secret service agent positioned himself in the row directly behind John and me to our right. In front, several agents also stood to the left and right of the speaker's podium. Agents also stood near the exit doors. Other agents stood about the room, and some agents stood in the back of the room, facing the podium.

Then, Vice President Pence's wife appeared, accompanied by a Secret Service agent. Because we were on the front row, they walked by us. The agent positioned the Vice President's wife three seats to our right. Walking behind her was her son and, I assume, the daughter. It could have been a daughter-in-law. I just did not know. When Vice President Pence initially began speaking, he, of course, introduced his wife. What was so endearing to observe was the son's facial expression while his mom stood and waved to the crowd. As she waved to the audience, the son's eyes never left her, and his eyes conveyed a very protective look for his mother. William Shakespeare said, "The eyes are the window to your soul." Because I was sitting so close to the Pence family, I witnessed this quote in action. Observing the son, I surmised he was ready to protect his mother at a moment's notice. You see notable people in the spotlight and in the news every day, but how often do we think about their family members? As I watched this young man, I perceived a family dynamic and a son's reverential love and respect for his mom. That was a very poignant moment! When Vice President Pence finished speaking, he left the stage, and his wife and the entourage were quickly whisked away by the Secret Service. Watching this family under the care of the Secret Service, I was reminded that we should all remember 1 Timothy 2:1–4 and the biblical command to pray for all in authority. They all need our prayers, even the Secret Service.

VALUES VOTER SUMMIT
WASHINGTON, DC - SEPTEMBER 2018

Another Surprise Meeting

At this 2018 Values Voter Summit, Vice President Pence was again the first scheduled speaker for the Friday morning event. We went through the usual FBI security check. After speaking, Vice President Pence left the podium, and John and I assumed, along with everyone else, that he had a tight schedule and had to leave. Many people left for lunch. However, John and I remained behind, visiting and talking to people. After a few minutes, the noise level in the room changed to a low roar. We looked toward the podium and noticed people were congregating near it. Vice President Pence and his Secret Service entourage had returned. We added ourselves to the greeting line that quickly formed. There were several Secret Service agents who stood out among the other agents because they were bald or had very little hair. While standing in line, John humorously asked the Secret Service agents near us if being bald was a prerequisite for being hired as an agent. A female agent standing directly in front of us quickly quipped, "Not me!"

Our line moved along, and we met Vice President Pence; I shook his hand and said, "I'm praying for you." He looked at me, nodded his head, and said, "Thank you."

I have watched Vice President Pence give interviews, and he has often said that he is encouraged to know that people are praying.

There were, of course, numerous Secret Service agents in the room. Generally, we do not think about the Secret Service agents and their well-being when we see them on TV or in other scenarios. They do their job and go wherever the president or vice president's schedule directs them. While standing there, I had the opportunity to converse with an agent. He mentioned to me that he had only *four* hours of sleep the night before. I can only assume he was on assignment. I felt sorry for him. This is just a reminder to all of us that Secret Service men and women need our prayers too.

Speaking to Vice-President Pence
as Secret Service agents stand nearby.

THE BIRTHING OF A PRAYER MOVEMENT IN SOUTHERN BRAZORIA COUNTY

Now 1Church1Day will be discussed. You ask, "What is 1Church1Day?" 1Church1Day is a prayer strategy that unites churches to pray a shared prayer guide that focuses on the pillars of society. The following gives background information on how it began and its purpose.

A POWERFUL PROVEN PRAYER STRATEGY

The birthing of a strategy: In his book *A Watchman's Guide to Praying God's Promises*, Dick Eastman tells the reader that:

> *In the mid-1970's, God drew two visionary leaders together for a luncheon meeting in Colorado; one leader was the founder of Campus Crusade for Christ, and the other leader was the founder of Youth with a Mission...each felt the Lord was revealing an important strategy...to impact nations and cultures...(in order) to initiate true transformation of a society. Little did they know (when meeting that) they both had*

*received the same insights…(and) a few weeks
later a well-known theologian received an
identical revelation.*

Eastman 2012, 23

What was this revelation? In the book, the author said they realized, "*To impact all of a culture…with the totality of the Gospel of Jesus Christ, every major sphere of influence had to be impacted.*"

What were the major spheres of influence? Family, church, government, business, education, healthcare, media, and arts/entertainment. In some instances, these spheres of influence are sometimes referenced as pillars of society and, in other instances, as mountains of society.

How was this strategy fulfilled? The author stated in his book, "*We pray from God's promises which is His answer (His word) and expect it to be fulfilled,*" according to 1 John 5:14–15.

Whatcom County, Washington State: In 2005, Whatcom County churches in Washington State united together to pray each month specifically for areas of culture by implementing a strategic prayer initiative to pray for their community and for the nation using specific scriptures in each sphere of influence.

At that time Whatcom County had a high crime rate. As churches prayed over time, the crime rate went down. The area also experienced a terrific fire, but the Lord's protection was on the first responders who were ambushed by a shooter at the scene of the fire. No one was hurt, and the details describing how each responder was protected from all the flying bullets were amazing!

An international 1Church1Day prayer movement: Internationally, 1Church1Day.org also has a website that gives insights about the impact of prayer strategy internationally. The founder of Kingdom League International has a blog in which he gives up-to-date information about this international prayer strategy. He even shared the example that prayer protected Christians in Myanmar (Burma) and India from a terrible attack. He said, "It's my sincerest hope and desire that other ministers would choose to adopt the 1Church1Day strategy, which is a modern application of an ancient blueprint first modeled by King David on Mt. Zion."

Now that you have an understanding about 1Church1Day's prayer strategy, you will marvel at how the Lord brought forth His plan for Brazoria County via prophecy.

PROPHETIC WORDS AND THEIR MEANING

Over the years I certainly did not understand some of the prophetic words I received because many of those words were about the *future*, but now in retrospect and after walking through those years and those events, I have a greater understanding of the meaning of those words, and many of the puzzle pieces have now "snapped into place. "

As you read the following prophetic words, you will marvel at God's plan that came to fruition over an expanse of time. Proverbs 16:9 (AMPC) says, "*A man's mind plans his way, but the Lord directs his steps and makes them sure.* "The Lord certainly directed my steps according to His plans.

FEBRUARY 19, 2001

The Initial Prophetic Word about God's Plan

On February 19, 2001, Evangelist Gary, a prophetic evangelist, uttered the first reference, the very first hint about God's future plan for Brazoria County. In fact, it was not until writing this book that I realized that this prophetic word was the beginning of God's plan for

1Church1Day. The word Evangelist Gary spoke to me that Sunday stated:

> "Rosamond, I saw the winds of change blowing through you. I saw you like a Holy Ghost windmill. I saw you like a Holy Ghost weathervane. And the Lord is going to speak to you and through you and show you things—which direction the wind of God is blowing in the city and even the whole county. I just saw the different directions of wind, and God is going to give you revelation, interpretation, and meaning of all that. And I see the tidal wave of the Holy Ghost, and God is getting ready to show you some things that are getting ready to hit America for good, and one of them is the tidal wave. Spiritually, you are going to see this tidal wave rise up so big, and it is just going to flood the United States of America. There is going to be a great purging that is going to take place. There is going to be a great deliverance that is going to work in people's lives. And I just saw you, though, like a Holy Ghost windmill...just blowing...just blowing."

The reference to knowing "which direction the wind of God is blowing in the city and even the whole county" was a part of God's long-term plan for Brazoria County; these words were spoken to me fifteen years before

1Church1Day even manifested onto the scene! Now, after rereading this word, I am amazed at its accuracy, clarity, and insight relating to Brazoria County and the Lord's plan for the county.

Also, on reflection, now I understand the Holy Spirit's words spoken to me in 2001 concerning the "different direction of the wind" that would be "blowing in Brazoria County" and even in our nation for aspects of society: family, government, healthcare, business, media, education, and the church. Additionally, with the words, "God is going to give you revelation, interpretation, and meaning of all that," I now realize this was a reference to the Holy Spirit downloading to me issues that needed to be addressed, scriptures that needed to be referenced about those events, and prayers that needed to be prayed to focus on the different spheres of society in the 1Church1Day prayer guide.

According to this word, Brazoria County would be the spiritual recipient of a "...tidal wave [that would] rise up so big, and it is just going to flood the United States of America." We have not seen this spiritual tidal wave yet; however, it is certainly a word of hope to counteract all the chaos we are observing in our nation and in our society today.

This prophetic word also stated, "There is going to be a great purging that is going to take place." The definition of *purging* is "a purification or a cleansing." According to this word, there is going to be a removal of some undesirable aspects of our culture. Hopefully, there will be a great tidal wave of a revival and a restoration of God's Spirit and His Word in America!

At the present time, 1Church1Day has forty participating churches uniting in prayer using the prayer guides. This unity is creating a spiritual canopy over our county to hopefully bring this prophetic word into fruition. We do not know for sure, but based on this prophetic word, an army of prayer warriors will have a great impact on our county, our state, and our nation. A tidal wave of righteousness has been prophesied to rise up and form over southern Brazoria County and be influence for the nation. That is exciting news!

DECEMBER 27, 2004
THREE YEARS LATER

Three years later, in 2004, I received a prophetic word that added more information about the Lord's plans for our county. This is an excerpt from the prophetic word from Christian International Ministries, which said:

> "Rosamond, I want you to be as one that builds up, and I want you to be one that restores

places. And I want you to be a rebuilder of the broken-down walls, not just in human being's lives but even in your very community of the broken-down walls as you network with other Christians, and even there is a networking with others in other fellowships, and it is not necessarily a church meeting, but it is a fellowship. It is causing the net to come together and each part to be knotted so that when the harvest of fish comes, none are lost."

I now realize that the references to "the *broken-down walls*" and to the "networking with others in fellowships" were part of the Lord's plan to unite churches and hearts together via the 1Church1Day prayer guides that the churches pray. The words "a rebuilder of the broken-down walls" reminds us of the biblical story about Nehemiah and the rebuilding of Jerusalem's broken-down walls. According to this prophetic word, 1Church/Day's united prayers will rebuild the broken-down walls and create a spiritual wall around Brazoria County and hopefully, our state and our nation.

This prophetic word also spoke about "a fellowship." This "fellowship" is a spiritual connection, a gathering of church partners, the ones who will be praying the prayer guides. We know this because the prophetic word spoke about "a networking" but "not necessarily a church meeting." The prayers prayed using the prayer guides are creating a spiritual umbrella over our county and a spiritual connection, unifying hearts. Isn't this amazing? The Lord has a specific plan for Brazoria County, and He gave glimpses via prophetic words little by little and over time.

JUNE 7, 2008
FOUR YEARS LATER

Four years later, in 2008, the Lord added even more information. At a meeting in Garland, Texas, a suburb of Dallas, Pastor Marijohn, whom I mentioned earlier in the book, prophesied more of the Lord's instructions about the future. Pastor Marijohn prophesied:

> "The Lord said, 'I am going to give you instructions. I am going to give you an understanding,' and He said, 'This is future.' He said, 'You are going to have it, and you're going to do it.' …It looks like the area has gone dry, very dry; it's very dry. It's like it's so dusty. It's very, very dry. He is going to use you to spearhead something that is going to bring the water of the Spirit into the area, and He said the place is not going to be dry anymore."

In this prophetic word, the Lord gave another tidbit of information about His plan. At the time I received this word, I was clueless as to its meaning. Evidently, our county had become spiritually very dry, and these churches, uniting in prayer, would be the "engine" for the Lord to "bring the water of the Spirit into the area," and a watering in the spiritual realm would take place because of prayers being prayed in our area.

In this prophetic word, there was also a mention of the word *spearhead*. The dictionary's definition of *spearhead* is "an individual or group chosen to lead an attack or movement." As you continue reading about 1Church1Day, you will see how the Lord brought Susan Moore and me together to spearhead this movement and direct the strategy to unite churches in prayer.

However, on June 7, 2008, those words were for the future; I was clueless as to their meaning. At that time, I only gleaned from this word that Brazoria County spiritually had become a very dry place.

JUNE 5, 2015
SEVEN YEARS LATER

Seven years later, on June 5, 2015, in Hurst, Texas, a suburb near Dallas, I attended Life Gate International

Church's Friday night service. I mentioned this
church earlier and the terrific training they do with
prophetic teams. On this Friday evening, I signed up
for a prophetic word. On that night, one team member
prophesied to me:

> "The Lord says, 'I'm going to connect your
> steps, and I'm sending you. I'm sending you,
> but I'm not going to send you out alone. There
> are some people that I'm going to connect you
> to that will continue to bring you up to that
> new level that I have called you to...' The Lord
> says, 'There are some things I want you to
> have. And you get to choose what those things
> are. You are going to look into that treasure
> chest, and you are going to pull–even as
> Esther was taken into that place, and she could
> choose whatever before the king. Daughter,
> I'm opening that treasure chest for you as you
> go out,' and the Lord says, 'Those doors are
> going to open...'"

At the time those words were about the future, and
they were a puzzlement to me. They were spoken *fifteen
years before* 1Church1Day even materialized on scene.
Now that 1Church1Day has been organized and set
in motion, the meaning of the words "There are some
people that I'm going to connect you to" makes sense

because this *connection* has occurred. This word was referring specifically to the Lord connecting Susan Moore and me together and the other participants—those who would be praying the 1Church1Day prayer guides.

Additionally, the meaning of the words "The Lord says, 'There are some things I want you to have. And you get to choose what those things are'" is also clear to me now. These words denote the times I will be reading, studying, and choosing prayer points and scripture applications for the various topics on the prayer guide. Sometimes the strategic team members send in scriptures to use with their prayer points; however, in many instances, I select the scriptures for each topic.

I always wondered about the meaning of the words "You are going to look into that treasure chest…" In retrospect, I now understand these words are referring to those times when I will be searching for appropriate scriptures to fit prayer points. I often search through my stacks of three-by-five-inches scripture cards to find an exact scripture to fit the prayer points for the prayer guide. Now I realize this "treasure chest" is referring to my scripture search among all my scripture cards, which are categorized according to topics. These are my "treasure chests."

One can only marvel at the Holy Spirit, these

prophecies, and their accuracy. Prophetic words concerning the future, of course, take time to unfold, to understand, and to perceive their revelation and their meaning. This is what happened to me; the revelation and puzzle pieces all came together and "snapped into place" as I wrote this book!

A TRIP TO SOUTH CAROLINA JULY 2015-ONE MONTH LATER

As I have already mentioned, my husband's hobby is growing citrus and other fruit-bearing trees. John is often asked to speak at nurseries in the Houston area and even out of state. Over the years he has developed what he humorously calls his "serious business." He has a website and a Facebook page where he gives information to help others to be successful in their fruit tree endeavors.

Because of my husband's avid fruit tree interest, we attend many fruit conferences. In 2015, we attended a conference in Charleston, South Carolina. When the conference ended, we decided to attend Morningstar Ministries' Sunday morning service. So, after the conference, we drove to Fort Mills, South Carolina. Morningstar Ministries operates a hotel called The Heritage Grand. It is the center for many facets of

Morningstar Ministries. In fact, church services take place on the main floor of the hotel. There are two Sunday morning services; John and I attended the eleven o'clock service. It was crowded, but we found some empty chairs at a table near the back. Instead of pews, Morningstar Ministries has round tables and chairs placed about the room.

On the day of our visit, two Morningstar ministers preached the Sunday message. One of the ministers, Pastor Robert, spoke on the topic "keys and principles to our prayers." I took notes while he spoke. One memorable comment he made was, "If you have a problem, ask the Lord; ask Him for strategies about what to do."

Then, a second minister, Pastor Perry, spoke after Pastor Robert. When Pastor Perry finished speaking, he began making decrees and declarations from the platform, and Pastor Robert simultaneously walked among the people sitting at the tables. As he walked about, Pastor Robert would stop and pray for various individuals or speak a prophetic word to them. I watched as he walked about the room.

Then, he walked to where John and I were sitting. He stopped, looked at me, and repeated three times, "Increase and comprehension. Increase and comprehension. Increase and comprehension." I had no idea what those words meant. After speaking to me, Pastor Robert then continued walking around to other tables, speaking here and there as the Holy Spirit prompted him.

Later, John asked me, "How did he know to speak to you?" John also commented that he thought Pastor Robert was going to put his hand on my shoulder, but then he did not. John added, "Maybe he hesitated because he did not know you."

The Holy Spirit is amazing! We were first-time visitors at a church service *in South Carolina*, and the Lord used this pastor, who was sensitive to the Holy Spirit, to speak a word to me. As I have stated, at that time I had no idea what the words "Increase and comprehension" meant. Now, in retrospect, I realize the Lord was informing me about a change that was pending. The change was on the horizon. Now, because I have walked through that time, so to speak, I understand the meaning of the words spoken to me, but at the time, I did not; I did not have a clue!

AUSTIN, TEXAS
AUGUST 26, 2015

On August 26, 2015, I attended a Christian conference at Arise Ministries in Austin, Texas. This ministry had organized prophetic teams to prophesy to the attendees. At this evening conference, I received the following word:

> "The Spirit of the Lord says, 'I'm bringing you up to a place where you have been seeking an end of a chapter; I see you are at the end of a chapter,' but the Spirit of the Lord says, 'As this new chapter is opening up for you, it's going to be such a place of adventure for you—a place of new, new, new things for you... I see you as a spokesperson for Me,' and the Lord says, 'You're one that would be able to draw others in even almost like a partner. I see you gathering people up and just speaking to them and just speaking directly into their hearts.'"

This word was spoken one year *before* 1Church/Day materialized onto the scene. In this prophetic word, there is a reference to an "end of a chapter." The Holy Spirit was signifying to me that an end of a chapter, an end of a season, was near, and this new chapter, this

259

new season, was approaching. This "newness" was emphasized with the words "new, new, new things." Like other words about the future, those words were a mystery to me at that time. I did not grasp their meaning because the "new" had not begun in my life. I now realize this reference to a "new chapter" was the reference to the 1Church1Day prayer movement. In this prophetic word, there is also a reference to being a "spokesperson" for the Lord.

As it turned out, Susan and I were the organizers to bring forth God's plan for the prayer movement. We were the spokespersons speaking for the Lord. The prayer guides were the tools the Lord would use and is still using to "speak directly" into *the hearts* of the people as they pray the prayer guides.

Also, the "gathering of people" would not be a literal gathering of individuals as a group as in a church setting, but it would be a spiritual gathering of participants who would be praying the prayer guides. In this word there is also a reference to the word *partner.* This same word had been spoken in previous prophetic words; this *partnership* was the connection of all the churches and their praying teams, working and coordinating in prayer together.

The second lady on the prayer team for Arise Ministries prophesied to me that:

> "I just hear a circle of influence. You are going to be influencing some people that you do not realize you are going to be influencing. And you have influenced some people in the past that you never realized, and the Lord is going to use you in that way. And this situation that He is going to bring you through is going to minister and speak to the people around you."

Again, this word revealed the Lord's plans for Brazoria County. Of course, I had no idea at the time of the meaning of "...influencing some people..." and also the words "...minister and speak to people all around you." All these words were alluding to the prayer participants who would be reading and praying the 1Church1Day prayer guides.

A BEE, NECTAR, AND REVELATION
AUGUST 27, 2015

The Arise Ministries conference continued into the next day. At one point at the conference, we were instructed to turn to someone and prophetically minister to them. On this day the Holy Spirit revealed more prophetic clues and pieces to the prophetic puzzle. Of course, I did not realize this fact at that time. The lady sitting next to me was on the ministry team at Summit Ministries in San Antonio; she prophetically said to me:

> "The Lord has given you a lot of revelation. I see it like a bee that gathers nectar. So there is a lot of nectar that the Lord has allowed you to gather, and He is going to begin to ring that revelation out of that nectar. There is new revelation coming, and as you pray, the Lord is going to show you. He's going to take you to a new level. The Lord is going to be able to use that revelation, that nectar, as a tool. It's going to be like a key that you're going to be able to unlock things that need to be unlocked. He is blowing upon that revelation and is taking you to that new level."

What was the meaning of the analogy of "bees and nectar"? Of course, this revelation, like the other references about the future, I did not understand at the time, but now I understand that the words "...a bee that gathers nectar" are a reference to my three-by-five-inches scripture cards that I have made over the years. As I have mentioned, I have numerous scripture cards that I have separated and classified according to prayer topics.

The words "...to ring that revelation out of that nectar" refer to the times I would be searching to find an exact scripture to "fit" a specific prayer point. Psalm 19:9–10 (NIV) refers to the sweetness of honey, stating, "*The decrees of the LORD are firm, and all of them are righteous. They are more precious than gold, than much pure gold; they are sweeter than honey from the honeycomb.*"

The words "bees," "nectar," "honey," and other prophetic words were just prophetic puzzle pieces to me at that time, but as I have shared, when I began rereading and pulling things together for this book, then the meaning became very clear. When I received this prophecy, the words *new level* were just like other prophetic words that I kept receiving. Because I have now *walked through* these events, this *new level* is now obvious to me.

A GOD-DIRECTED DREAM
FEBRUARY 2, 2016

At one point, Sharlene, a friend who has Bible study meetings in her home, asked me if I would teach a Bible lesson for the ladies at one of the Sunday evening sessions in her home. That evening, I had the following dream.

The dream: In this dream for some reason, I had to have my license renewed. Somehow the renewal of my license related to the school where I had taught. I entered a room at the school, and there were a lot of people in it. I said to myself, "Well, where do I go to get my license renewed?" I walked around, looking. Then I went to a table where I recognized a former teacher that I knew; however, the person who shared this teacher's room came up to me at that moment and asked, "How can I help you?" I had brought a folder with me, and I began looking into it for my license. Somehow, I had forgotten my license. The lady then looked in my folder at my papers, and then she said to me, "Your license has almost expired." So, I told her that I would go home and get my license and come right back. That was the end of the dream.

Diane, an intercessor and a friend, is gifted in interpreting dreams. It's truly a gift the Lord has given her. I sent my dream to her to see what spiritual insight she might have about it because the dream was certainly a puzzlement to me. She did an excellent job of analyzing the dream's content. Following is Diane's interpretation of the dream.

The Interpretation of the Dream

The purpose of a license: A car license is something you need to be able to go anywhere since you cannot drive a car without one. In the dream, your license represents your independence because you can go and do what God has called you to do. You can "ride" with other people, but then you must depend on them, which greatly restricts what you can do. This "license" represents the ability God has given you to do what He has called you to do.

The expiring license: In your dream, your license has almost expired. God is calling you to do something different than what you have been doing. He wants to renew what He has given you, and He wants to give you fresh, new abilities to accomplish the new things He has for you. If you do not get these new abilities and these downloads, then you will be greatly restricted from crossing over into the new things that God has for you.

The new wineskin: In your dream, "going to school" represents going back to the familiar things that you have been doing and are competent in doing—in the natural or in the spiritual. The teacher in the dream represents someone from the past (the old, the familiar equals the old wineskin) who said your license had almost expired. In other words, the old, familiar things you have done are about to expire, and you are about to walk into a new assignment—a new wineskin.

The new versus the old: You had to go home and get your license and return.

The new: You will take all that you have learned in the past (going home) into the new season with you, but it will not be used in the same way because God is doing something *new* in you, and some of the *old* is not needed anymore. Some of the people in the *old* may also not go with you into the *new*.

The forgetting: All the forgetting (not having the license) may mean hesitancy on your part to go with the *new,* but you are still going forward anyway.

This is the end of the dream analysis.

Commentary: I had totally forgotten about this dream when I was planning this book; however, I was looking through my prophetic words while writing this book, and I came upon this dream and Diane's interpretation. At that time, I was somewhat hesitant to tell Sharlene that I would not be able to share a Bible study lesson with the study group. This dream confirmed the Lord had something else for me to do.

A revelation: When I reread Diane's analysis, I

checked the date and the year. I then realized that God's plan to initiate 1Church1Day was fast approaching on His calendar.

As you read the following prophecies, you will see my prophetic words becoming more specific as the Lord sets in motion His plans for southern Brazoria County.

THREE MONTHS LATER
APRIL 25, 2016

For many years a group of ladies gathered weekly in my home to pray for our nation, our state, and our local city government, and occasionally, we would gather to pray and prophetically seek insights from the Lord concerning the group. At one of these sessions, Joyce, a friend and an intercessor, spoke a prophetic word to me. In an excerpt from this word, Joyce said, "It's like I see you overseeing; you're an overseer. It is like a pyramid; I don't know...but it will not be called a pyramid..."

This "pyramid" reference described a symbolic structure for how the churches would be organized to pray the 1Church1Day prayer guides. It would not literally be a pyramid. These words were an analogy describing what Joyce was sensing in the spiritual realm, a connection of the future churches united under the 1Church1Day prayer canopy.

This word, *overseer*, hints at Susan's and my role as *overseers* of 1Church1Day for Brazoria County. In the 1Church1Day structure, there are strategic team leaders who are experienced in their field of expertise. They send in prayer points every two months concerning their area of expertise for the family, national government, state/county government, healthcare, business, media, education, and the church.

My intercessory friend, Diane, teamed prophetically with Joyce and added the following:

> "You know you're an organizer...and God says, 'I'm fixing to use those skills even more...for citywide things and organizing accessory groups for this, and it will not be a burden... So just get ready, and you're going to get a call from someone you thought you'd never get a call from. And they are going to ask you to do something like that, and you are going to think, Lord, can I do something like that? ...So just get ready for that!'"

The reference to "citywide things" refers to the connection of churches to the prayer guides and the prayer topics. The reference to "organizing accessory groups" is a reference to uniting each church to choose a day of the month to pray the prayer guides.

Diane mentioned the idea of "a call." This was the telephone conversation the Lord planned for Susan and me. Susan Moore was the "someone you thought you'd never get a call from." Susan and I knew each other but not well. In this word, the Holy Spirit was signaling to me to be on the alert for a phone call; it was coming!

Conclusion: Isn't this amazing? The Lord used many prophetic words as a tool to reveal His overall plan for uniting churches in prayer for Brazoria County.

ABOUT THREE WEEKS LATER
MAY 16, 2016

On May 16, 2016, the director of prayer at KSBJ, a Houston Christian radio station, came to Lake Jackson Civic Center because Pastor Cedric, head of the Baptist Ministerial Association, had invited him to speak. Pastor Cedric said he did not have any idea what the director of prayer at KSBJ would speak about; however, those in attendance that evening listened, and the director spoke about 1Church1Day, an effortless way for churches to pray together for the community, the state, and our nation in strategic and relevant ways. As stated, 1Church1Day was initiated in Washington State. In Houston, the suburbs of Humble, Kingwood, and Atascocita adopted this church prayer strategy. At the May 16th meeting, the KSBJ prayer director explained 1Church1Day, a strategic model of sustainable twenty-four-seven prayer uniting churches without physically meeting together. Each participating church was to choose one day out of the month to pray for twenty-four hours. The KSBJ director of prayer explained that 1Church1Day creates a church-led, year-round prayer strategy. At the meeting, Pastor Cedric appointed Susan Moore to head up the endeavor. About seventy Christians were at the meeting, and sample prayer guides were passed out for everyone to peruse.

On the following Wednesday, Susan met with her weekly prayer partners; one of the men in the group said to her, "Susan, you cannot do this by yourself. This is too big of a project for one person." Later, Susan told me that when those words were spoken to her, my name immediately came into her mind. During my prayer time on that same Wednesday morning, I reread the sample prayer guide that was passed out at the meeting, and I thought to myself, *Perhaps I could help Susan*; then I thought, *I will call Susan*, but I hesitated, paused for a moment, and said to myself, *No, if the Lord wants me to do this, Susan will call me.* About fifteen minutes later, the phone rang! Susan called me! We can only marvel at the Lord's timing!

Susan and I then began to strategize how to bring 1Church1Day into fruition. She began contacting pastors, and she and I visited numerous pastors, informing them about 1Church1Day. Susan had been the owner of *Sonshine Bookstore*, and because of that fact, she knew a lot of pastors.

Buddy Scott, director of His Love, a Christian counseling service, wrote an article in *The Facts,* our local paper, about 1Church/Day for his weekly column. Susan told me that she reads his column every Saturday. When one of his articles came out in *The Facts*, Susan called me, asking if I had read it. I had not, so I found *The Facts* and perused the article. Buddy Scott wrote a delightful article describing how he had met Susan in her bookstore when he was searching for some biblical study material. Susan gave him several books and a CD for him to begin this project. Buddy Scott also interwove in this article the strategy and purpose of the new adventure for our area—the prayer initiative.

ONE MONTH AND TEN DAYS LATER
JUNE 29, 2016

In his book *Prophets and Personal Prophecy*, Dr. Hamon said that prophetic words usually give general information about our lives, but he said when the Lord's purpose is imminent and close to materializing for an individual, then their prophetic words become more specific and more instructive. As I studied and pieced together date by date my prophetic words, I was able to see how these prophetic words were truly moving from general to specific information.

On June 29, 2016, Dr. Hamon's ministry sent me a prophetic word that gave me specific instructions. The Holy Spirit was alerting me to be on the lookout for what the Lord would be doing; the prophetic word stated:

> "Father God, I thank You that You're moving in a fresh and new way... I heard the Lord say, 'Daughter, watch what I'm going to do.' He said, 'Watch!' He said, 'It's time to start to put a watchful eye out and start looking over the horizon. Even as Elijah's servant would go to the top of the mountain to see what was coming, and though he went seven times, it was not until the seventh time that he looked and that he saw the cloud the size of a man's

hand… I'm shifting things and time. I'm
shifting things around in a new and fresh way…
I am the One that caused the doors to open
before you in fresh and new ways.' I see God
showing you some things in the future that are
going to just come upon you very quickly…
He said, 'Because I am the one who set up the
timing. I am the One that caused the doors to
open before you in a fresh, new way.'"

In this prophetic word, there was the reference again
to the "new" and the fact that the Lord was moving in
a "new way." The Holy Spirit also instructed me to be
on the "lookout." The Holy Spirit also said to "put a
watchful eye out and start looking over the horizon."
Webster's definition of the word *horizon* is something
that is "happening very soon."

One way to authenticate a prophetic word is to see
biblical references in it. In this prophetic word, there was
a reference to the prophet Elijah and "a cloud the size of
a man's hand." This is a biblical story about Elijah and his
servant. As you read 1 Kings 18:42–44 (AMPC), you can
see how this prophetic word parallels very closely to the
biblical story about Elijah and his servant:

> *So, Ahab went up to eat and drink. And Elijah*
> *went up to the top of Carmel; and he bowed*
> *himself down upon the earth and put his face*

between his knees. And said to his servant, Go up now, look toward the sea. And he went up and looked and said, There is nothing. Elijah said, Go again seven times. And at the seventh time, the servant said, A cloud as small as a man's hand is arising out of the sea. And Elijah said, Go up, say to Ahab, hitch your chariot and go down, lest the rain stop you.

I was instructed to "watch" and to have "a watchful eye" for God's plan to come forth. This was specific! Like Elijah, I was told to "start looking over the horizon" and…"to put a watchful eye out" and "to watch the horizon."

THE LAUNCHING
SEPTEMBER 1, 2016

On September 1, 2016, the first 1Church1Day prayer guide was sent out to all the participating churches in southern Brazoria County. Initially, Susan and I met with pastors, "gathering together" those churches who would pray the 1Church1Day prayer guides. As churches pray the 1Church1Day prayer guides, the Holy Spirit unites our hearts, creating a positive spiritual climate over southern Brazoria County. This was exactly the Lord's plan. One of the prophetic words that I referenced earlier was that our area had "become dry—very dry." With all the churches uniting in prayer, we are creating unity in the spiritual realm and a spiritual canopy over our area, counteracting "the dryness" of the past.

PROPHETIC WORDS

Prophetic words are not spoken in a linear fashion of first, second, and third, etc., and many times they are often clouded in spiritual clues. Sometimes we think we understand a prophetic word and the Lord's purpose, but as time progresses, we realize that what we thought a prophetic meant was not what the Lord meant, but all during this time, the Lord continues working in our hearts, cleaning us up and preparing us for His purpose and plan.

Often prophetic words need the passage of time, prayer, and contemplation on our part for God's plan to manifest in our hearts and into the physical realm. This is especially true if a prophetic word concerns the future. What would be the purpose of receiving a prophetic word about the future if we readily understood everything that would take place? Also, the Lord encases our prophetic words in a type of mystery so that we walk by faith, trusting Him.

THE INCREASE

Through the years the 1Church1Day prayer guides have been sent out to the churches and their volunteers to pray. When the prayer movement first began, there were thirty-one participating churches; now, there are forty. People have often told Susan Moore and me that because of information and prayers presented in the prayer guide, they have become more aware of candidates' names, of those running for office, and of leadership decisions and important positions in local, state, and national issues. Others have shared that they use the prayer guides during their daily prayer time as a guide for their prayers.

A TRIPPING
A REPEAT PERFORMANCE

In August of 2018, I made an appointment to update my pastor about the 1Church1Day prayer initiative. The office secretary walked me to the pastor's office, but the minute I stepped over the threshold into his office, my ankles involuntarily *flickered*! I nearly lost my balance, but I was able to recover my steps and thus stopped a potential fall. This was the same flickering motion that I shared earlier with the reader when I fell on the sidewalk near my home in 1993. Only at that time I did experience an unexpected fall.

When I stumbled, I am sure my pastor just thought I must have slipped on something or experienced a misstep. What was happening in the spiritual realm? I can only assume that the enemy was trying to discourage me.

TILLING THE SOIL

In March 1, 2019, we visited our daughter in Austin, and I again attended Arise Ministries' Friday evening service. They often give prophetic words for those in attendance. Following is an excerpt of the prophetic word spoken to me on that day:

> "The Lord says, 'That what you are doing as a ground intercessor—you're tilling the ground. You're tilling the ground with your prayers, and you are preparing the ground so that He can come and pour rivers of life in it (our area) to cause the life to come out of the ground that you are tilling. You are fertilizing it (our area) with your words.'"

I have previously mentioned that Pastor Marijohn prophesized years ago about the Brazoria County area and the fact that it had become *dry*. In fact, she said that the area had become *very dry*. She even stated that the area was "very dusty."

In contrast to this prophetic word about a "dryness," the prayers of the forty churches are "tilling the ground" and "fertilizing" the ground with the prayers of the volunteers reading and praying the 1Church1Day prayer guides. Evidently, sometime in the future, southern Brazoria County will have an even greater spiritual influence and impact not only on our area but also across the nation.

INTERCESSORS FOR AMERICA (IFA)

In October 2021, Intercessors for America (IFA) sent out an email requesting an opportunity to interact with intercessors in a virtual town hall meeting hosted by David Kubal, president/CEO of IFA. IFA periodically contacts individuals in various regions of the United States with the purpose of interacting with intercessors for discussion and focused prayer. I have been a supporter of IFA for many years, so I responded to IFA's email. I received a subsequent email inquiring if I would be available for a phone conversation with IFA and its staff members. The email stated there would be perhaps ten people on the phone call from our region. On the designated day of the call, other possible participants were busy, but I was free and available. Dave Kubal was gracious to take the time to speak to me, and because of a scheduled meeting, he passed the conversation on to his staff. The staff discussed IFA's goals and asked various questions relating to IFA and my interaction with their resources, services, etc. Following this aspect of the conversation, the IFA staff asked me, "What are you doing in your area?" I shared with them about 1Church1Day. They inquired about its purpose and how it had begun. My reply was that it would be much easier and more expedient of their time if I emailed them some information. I sent background information about how two visionary leaders, one, the leader of Campus Crusade for Christ, and the other leader, the founder of Youth with a Mission, plus a third person, a well-known leading theologian, had each received the same insight from God—the importance of impacting our culture with the gospel in all areas of society: the family, church, business, government, education, healthcare, media, and arts/ entertainment with God's promises. I also sent IFA a sample prayer guide so they could see the prayer format of 1Church1Day's prayer guide for the family, church, business, government, education, healthcare, media, and arts/entertainment.

In response to my email, one of IFA's contributing writers, Suni Piper, contacted me, and we planned a second phone conversation with Susan Moore and me. Next, Suni Piper and Judy McDonough interviewed Susan and me on a zoom call discussing 1Church1Day—how it began, how it operates, and how we compile information for the monthly prayer guide. Suni Piper then emailed me that an article would appear about 1Church1Day in IFA's magazine, *The Connecter*, and another article would appear in IFA's online magazine, *The Informer*. IFA is a wonderful organization promoting prayer for our nation. All we can say is, "Wow! Look at what the Lord did!"

I have taken you on this journey to show you how the Lord brought forth His plans for 1Church1Day and how accurate prophetic words can be in our lives. Now, other topics will be discussed.

A STRONG IMPRESSION

About twenty years ago, during my prayer time, I received a strong impression: I saw myself speaking before a large group of people. This impression was so real to me that I shared it with my pastor, Pastor Logan at that time, with Pastor Janette, and with several close friends. Because it was such a long time ago, I had forgotten about this impression. However, in 2017, I attended, along with Susan Moore and Mary Leveron, three meetings in the Houston area to hear a speaker inform the audience about Loving Houston, a school-church program. In this program the speaker shared how some Houston churches had partnered with some school districts in a myriad of ways to help students be more successful. Using Loving Houston as a prototype, the three of us worked together to organize Loving BISD for our area. I created documents on the computer and made graphs and diagrams to illustrate the church-school partnership concept. Mary Leveron contacted the superintendent of Brazosport Independent School District (BISD) and asked for permission to initiate a Loving BISD program for our area. Susan contacted numerous churches, informing them of the pending meeting to discuss this church-school partnership program. Many pastors and ministry leaders attended.

The superintendent of our school district (BISD) opened the meeting with prayer and prayed that the Lord would help the churches become partners with our local schools. He gave an overview of BISD's accomplishments and goals and concluded his presentation with four scriptures.

Next, Susan Moore spoke to those in attendance about Loving Houston and how it worked in the Houston area. Then, I focused on how a Loving BISD program could work with churches in our area. When I finished speaking, I turned to hand the microphone to the person in charge of BISD's technology, but Susan immediately asked me, "Are you going to talk about what you mentioned to me earlier?" I retrieved the microphone, turned, and said, "I just want to say one more thing. I want everyone to understand how fortunate we are to have our present BISD superintendent because he was receptive to the school-church program, and he immediately supported the idea of a BISD church-school partnership program." I stopped and looked at the audience and interjected, "You tell me how many superintendents would open a meeting by leading everyone in prayer *himself* and then end his presentation highlighting four *scripture verses*!" What was the audience's reaction? There was an immediate outburst of applause!

A few days after this meeting, the Holy Spirit brought to my remembrance the impression I had received *twenty years earlier* where I had seen myself standing before a large group of people. I had totally forgotten about this past impression! Ecclesiastes 3:1 (AMPC) says, "To everything there is a season and a time for every matter...," and the time and the season for me to understand this impression was in 2017. This was the *season* the Holy Spirit brought this impression into reality.

A TRIP TO ISRAEL
A MEMORABLE EVENING

Family Research Council (FRC) organized a trip to Israel in March-April 2018. John and I decided to join the trip. There were so many people on the tour that FRC had three buses with three tour guides. The second evening in Israel, the president of FRC arranged for two pastors to speak to our group after dinner. One speaker was a former Palestinian Muslim, and the other speaker was an Israeli Jew. They both had become Christians. What is so remarkable is that both men are now pastors of Christian churches in Israel, and both are good friends: Pastor Saleem, pastor of Home of Jesus King Church in Nazareth, Israel, and Pastor Daniel, pastor of Peniel Fellowship in Tiberias, Israel. They both spoke. Both of their stories were interesting, but Pastor Daniel's story was so dramatic and riveting about how Jesus intervened in his life that I wanted to share it with you.

Pastor Daniel's story centered on how the Lord saved his life, but I did not recall all the details. I remembered that he said he had authored a book about his life, so I emailed his church's website in Israel, asking to purchase his book. His wife responded to me; she said his book had been published in Hebrew and German but not in English. About two weeks later, I was surprised because Pastor Daniel's wife emailed me again, but this time she sent an English translation of the portion of the story that the pastor had shared with our tour group that evening.

I remember Pastor Daniel telling our group that he had accepted Jesus in his heart and became a Messianic Jew at the age of seventeen. He also said that when he told his father he had accepted Jesus as his Messiah, he thought his father was going to throw him out of the house. However, pausing for a moment, he added, "I'm grateful that did not happen."

Background Information— ### Israel's Military Requirements

In Israel when you graduate from high school, everyone is required to serve in the military. Girls are required to serve for two years and boys for three, and if you are accepted in their pilot training school, a pilot is required to stay in the military for nine years. Everyone in Israel serves in the military, but exceptions are given to individuals who are blind, handicapped, or have a severe illness.

Pastor Daniel's Story

During the whole time of my army service, the hand of the Lord was with me and kept me safe. In one incident, without a doubt, it was the hand of the Lord that saved my life.

Due to tension on our northern border with Syria, the unit I was serving was brought up from Sinai to be reinforcements for our forces on the Golan Heights (the northern part of Israel, a strategic location for Israel's defense). A short time after we were installed at the military base, which was located near the Druze village, Mas'ade, a night-time troop exercise commenced. We left the base on an armored personnel carrier and drove over to an area that had agricultural terraces that were located on a hilly terrain that was unfamiliar to us. (Agricultural terraces are methods of growing crops on sides of hills or sides of mountains. Terraces consist of ridges and channels constructed *across the sides* of hills or mountains.)

I sat in the armored vehicle on an elevated seat in which my upper body was positioned outside the opening of the soldier's compartment on the roof of the vehicle. In front of me in the commander's cell spot stood a veteran sergeant who was a seasoned tank commander, and his job was to direct the driver. Because I was sitting directly behind him, I did not have a good line of vision for the direction in front of us. To my right stood the troop's communication officer, whose upper body was exposed above the roof of the carrier. The armored personnel carrier proceeded without any lights. There was utter darkness. The moon had not risen yet, and the stars were hidden by clouds. Our night vision equipment that we used was antiquated and of truly little help. The little light that did illuminate onto the map that was in front of me completed my inability to see the way ahead.

We continued moving in the armored tank on a narrow road, heading toward the direction of the ramps that were on the eastern side of the mountain. *Suddenly, the still, small voice of the Lord spoke to my heart and warned me that we were in danger of turning over!* The sense of imminent danger caused me to warn the whole crew on the armored carrier's internal radio. I alerted them that we needed to watch out because we were in danger of overturning. I added that there were agricultural terraces on the slopes in the area, so we needed to be careful.

The driver stopped the armored vehicle and remarked that he could not see the way ahead. The navigator, who sat in the command cell, stated with confidence that he could see the way forward, and he directed us to continue. The driver was uncertain what to do and did not move because of the pitch-black darkness, and he could not see the way ahead. The navigator of the tank confidently repeated that he could see the way. Three times he gave the order to continue forward. Our communication officer, who had received the final orders from the troop commander before our night-time exercise had begun, also told the driver to move forward and proceed. The confidence in which the navigator spoke tipped the scale, and the driver began to slowly move us forward. I decided to obey the warning that I had received in my heart, and I began to prepare myself as we had been trained in case of the overturning in an armored carrier to go inside the vehicle and hold tight.

As soon as I started sliding downward, the armor personnel carrier started leaning inward, tipping at a sharp angle. The driver tried to apply the brakes to the slowly crawling vehicle, but this action was too late, and it only exacerbated the situation. The armored carrier fell over on its nose into a large pit and landed on its roof.

At that moment I found myself upside down on my head. Just a moment before, the sky had been above me, but in another moment, the ground was over my head. The cases of ammunition that were in the armored tank came loose. The machine gun also came loose from its moorings, along with heavy boxes of ammunition. They were all flying around inside the vehicle. The stench of death was in the air! I cannot explain it, but I felt at that moment that some men on the tank had been killed.

The results of the accident were deadly and tragic. The navigator of the carrier, who had just stood in front of me a few moments before, was now dead! Because his upper body was outside the vehicle, he had not been able to get inside the vehicle in time and was crushed to death!

Our communication officer, who had stood near me just a moment before, had evidently tried to jump out of the tank while it was overturning, but he did not make it. The lower part of his body was crushed under the heavy weight of the vehicle. I immediately called the troop commander on the radio network and told him what had happened. Our efforts to dig under the armored tank to rescue this officer failed. To my great sorrow, our troop's communication officer did not survive his injuries. He died in the helicopter on the way to the hospital. It took several hours before a crane arrived to lift and upright the heavy carrier.

Among all the soldiers who were partly outside the tank and above the roof of the tank, I was the only one who survived. There were also four other soldiers who were inside the vehicle who survived. *If God had not warned me, and if I had not responded immediately to His warning, I would not be alive today*. No karate exercise could have lifted the tons of iron the armored carrier weighed off of me. *I owe my life to God*!

When my father heard about the accident, he went to the Jewish synagogue and said a Birkat HaGomel to bless God for saving my life. (A Birkat HaGomel is a blessing for coming through trauma and prevailing; it is a Jewish prayer of gratitude to God.)

The Conclusion of the Evening

As we all sat on the terrace that evening listening to Pastor Daniel's riveting story and Pastor Saleem's insights, we were all spellbound. It was a memorable evening listening to these two pastors talk about their lives. Pastor Daniel even apologized for taking so much time speaking because he wanted to leave some time for his pastor friend. The atmosphere on the terrace was one of love, warmth, and peace. The Holy Spirit was certainly a guest at this gathering. As we were dispersing, John and I happened to walk by the president of Family Research Council; he was standing near the guest's table. I told him that this was a memorable evening for everyone. He nodded his head and said, "That's good to hear."

This was a wonderful memory of our trip—to hear two pastors in Israel who love Christ share their stories with everyone.

A CONNECTION WITH A FORMER STUDENT

In 2019, on Sunday morning, Susan Moore and I attended Willow Church's eight o'clock Sunday service. Pastor Scot was out of town, and a missionary couple, Shannon and her husband, were the guest speakers. Willow Church sponsors this couple's ministry endeavors in Botswana. The wife spoke to the congregation and explained that last time when they had visited the church, her husband had spoken, but this time she would be the speaker and inform everyone about their work with the youth in Botswana. After speaking, Lindsay and her husband were asked to come forward for prayer. One of the church leaders summoned several people to step forward to pray for the couple. A deacon then motioned for Susan Moore to join the group. While standing by the couple, Susan turned, looked at me in the congregation, and motioned for me to join them.

We each took turns praying for the couple. I remembered praying for the couple about their ministry, their children, and the youth of Botswana who were under their leadership. While praying, however, I received an impression; I saw the number–*one hundred*. I sensed that I was to contribute one hundred dollars to this couple's ministry. When the service was over, Susan and I joined the couple at an information table that had been set aside for them. It was at this point that the wife, Lindsay, told me that she was a former student of mine. She said she had been in my Bible history class at the high school. She added that she remembered the assigned projects for the ark of the covenant and the Ten Commandments, and she mentioned other projects too. She told me that as I walked forward to join the group in front to pray for them, she had said to herself, *I know that lady*. I did not recognize her; she shared with me that she had been a blonde in high school. She turned to her husband and said, "This was my teacher for my Bible history class."

At that point I realized why I had received the impression—the number *one hundred.* I told Shannon I wanted to give her something; I proceeded to write a check for one hundred dollars and told her to use the money for something that she really wanted or needed.

Later, when Susan and I returned to the car, I told Susan about my impression and seeing the number *one hundred.* She commented to me that while she was standing in the front with the couple, she just sensed that I should be included in praying for them. Isn't it remarkable how the Holy Spirit works!

A NEW AND UNEXPECTED ASSIGNMENT

On March 4, 2016, we were visiting our daughter in Austin, so I attended Arise Ministries' Friday night services again. During the service, the pastor spoke a prophetic word to me; he prophesied:

> "The Lord says, 'You have cried out and said, "Lord, I want to know You in a more excellent way."' And God says, 'I am going to show you that excellent way,' but the Lord says, 'That excellent way may not be exactly what you think it is. It might come at you from a whole other angle...'"

Because this word alluded to the future, I had no idea what the words "It might come at you from a whole other angle..." meant.

A NEW APPOINTMENT

Time passed, and on December 20, 2016, Dr. Hamon's ministry team sent me another prophetic word. In this word, the words "a *new day and a new appointment*" were mentioned. An excerpt of this word stated:

> *"God says, 'It's a new day, a new day, a new appointment that I have assigned to you... Things are preparing you for a new season— for a new day.' God says, 'It is a new day. A new day—a new appointment that I have assigned to you.' God says, 'Breakthrough, breakthrough, breakthrough in everything I have called you to do...' God says, 'I'm going to bring connections to you—divine appointments and opportunities to you...'"*

The other team member also gave more information about the *new*.

> *"'This is a season when you are going to begin to see (that) the old leaves have fallen off the tree.' God says, 'As I move the old leaves*

*away, you are going to see that things are
made new.' God says, 'The fall season is over.'
The Lord says, 'I am moving you even back
into a spring season. I am jumping you into a
whole new season. I am birthing and stirring
new ideas, and a new vision is coming forth
inside of your heart,' so God says, 'Get ready
for more. Get ready for the new as I shift you
into this new place in 2017.'"*

A NEW PLACE

I continued receiving prophetic words about the
new. On October 6, 2017, I again attended the Arise
Ministries services in Austin. An excerpt from the
ministry team's word to me stated, "...the Lord says He
is going to cause you to take a step farther into a new
place, not only in the spiritual realm but also in the
natural realm."

The theme about something *new* was also mentioned
by my insightful, intercessory friend Joyce. On January
22, 2018, Joyce prophesized to me:

"What I see about you is you are sitting at
your computer...and you are just sitting there,
and you're waiting on the Lord...and it's
something new. It is something straight from

the throne of heaven. It will be a certain time when you can just sit and wait on the Lord. It's something new...and so anointed that the enemy can't touch it."

SOMETHING NEW

The theme of something "new" seemed to be repeated in whatever prophetic word I received. On February 9, 2018, Celebration Ministries held a conference in Houston. They had prophetic teams at the conference. With this prophetic word, I also received a reference to something *new*. One of the ladies on the prophetic team prophesied to me:

> "...the Lord says, 'Do not be resistant to My instructions. I will show you where to go and how to go, and I will break open for you things you may have never seen before or done before. That it is a new thing—a new thing—that I am doing.' He said, 'Do not be confused, but just stay tight with Me.' He is going to give you some different instructions for different seasons. 'My daughter, I'm doing something new in the area of ministry for you.'"

At that specific moment, I thought to myself, *Why*

would I be resistant to the Lord's instructions? I could not understand why I was told to "…not to be resistant to the Lord's instructions." That was a real mystery to me because I have always tried to be obedient to the Lord and prophetic words spoken to me.

A NEW CHALLENGE

At another time, Joyce, my friend, was at my home with other ladies for a prayer meeting. At one point, Joyce stopped, looked at me, and said, "Just before I left home, I said, 'Lord, do you have a word for Rosamond?' He said, 'Yes, tell her I have a new challenge coming to her…'" She continued and said to me, "You won't have to worry. You will not have to fear. You will not have to think twice about it because He is going to let you know. There is a new challenge coming, and it is going to be great! This is a new challenge…" Again, I was clueless at that time as to the meaning of this word.

AN UNDERSTANDING OF THE "SOMETHING NEW"

Even though I received all these clues about something *new* from 2016 to 2018, I had no idea what the *new* implied. The timing of the new and the Lord revealing His specific plans for the *new* did not materialize until September 2019 at a Christian conference where I was given a clear directive to write a book! This was the new assignment! I shared with the reader at the beginning of the book that writing a book was not even close to "my wish list" of things to do!

This conference was held at Life International Church in Houston, as I mentioned at the beginning of this book. Besides speakers, the church organized prophetic teams to prophesy to the attendees. The pastor's daughter prophesied to me what I shared in the introduction on page 9. As a review, the prophetic word stated:

> "Rosamond, I hear the Spirit of the Lord saying, 'My daughter, I'm doing something new in the area of ministry for you...I'm bringing you into a higher place. I'm the One that is exalting you and promoting you in this season. There have been some words that you have felt in your spirit. There have even been thoughts about the desire of writing, even your own book.' The Lord says, 'I've birthed that idea within you...'"

In retrospect I now understand why I was instructed to "...not to be resistant to the Lord's instructions." And what happened when I was given this prophetic word? *Yes, I was resistant to* the Lord's instructions as I shared with the reader but only momentarily! The prophetic words spoken to me at Arise Ministries that "It might come at you from a whole other angle..." came to fruition! The thought of writing a book certainly came at me from "a whole other angle."

GOD'S PURPOSE AND PROPHESY

There are scriptures that reveal to us that God has a plan for every individual and God cares about each person. For instance, Proverbs 19:21 (AMPC) says, *"Many plans are in a man's mind, but it is the Lord's purpose for him that will stand."* This is one of the numerous scriptures that underscore God's design for our lives. The Lord's purpose and plans for individuals are also expressed in Ephesians 2:10 (NIV), which says, *"For we are God's handiwork, created in Christ Jesus to do good works which he has prepared in advance for us to do."* God has plans for each one of us that He designs well in advance! God knows every door that needs to open and every avenue we should take. We just need to be responsive to His promptings, His calling, and His prophetic words.

Years ago, Pastor Chester was a guest speaker at a Sunday evening church service I attended. While speaking, he made some interesting points about prophecy, how it works, and how God uses prophecy. I took notes as he spoke, and over the years, I have read, reread, and pondered his words. Pastor Chester said:

"Prophecy is like a mustard seed; it is exceedingly small and looks like nothing is going to happen." He continued and said, "Prophecy is similar to a promise, and a promise equals potential. Prophecy reveals our potential; we just have to be obedient to God and His plans for our lives for that potential to manifest in lives." Pastor Crutchfield went on to say, "With prophecy, God births something in your heart, and it has potential. Prophecy is your potential." He added, "We should wage a good warfare over prophecies that are spoken to us and stand." In this instance, the words *to stand* mean that an individual should pray over his prophetic words, persevere, and continue to follow the Lord so that those prophetic words do manifest in his life.

So God uses prophetic words to release His plans into our hearts. We may not completely understand the words when they are spoken, but little by little and year after year, we gain insight into those prophetic words and their meaning as the Holy Spirit brings forth revelation in our hearts. Prophetic words are our navigation system, our special GPS, guiding, directing,

PROPHECY: GOD'S POSITIONING SYSTEM FOR OUR LIVES

and encouraging us in the purpose and direction God has set aside for us.

My friend, Kathy Sanders, whom I mentioned earlier in the book, made a profound statement about prophecy. In an email to me, she wrote an excellent definition of prophecy. She said, "Honestly, I don't think any of us truly grasp the importance of prophecy. It is our history written in advance. It is God standing in the future, looking back to us in the present, and telling us what is coming."

In conclusion, I hope pastors and individuals allow the Holy Spirit to flow in church services so that prophetic words are birthed and continue to reside in people's hearts. Hearing prophetic words spoken in a church service or in a prayer meeting encourages individuals. Hopefully, these individuals, inspired by the Holy Spirit, will heed God's call for their lives.

BIBLIOGRAPHY

Bennett, Dennis, and Rita. *The Holy Spirit and You*. Plainfield: Logos International, 1971.

DeCamp, Harry S. *One Man's Healing from Cancer*. Old Tappan: Fleming H. Revell Company, 1983.

Eastman, Dick. *A Watchman's Guide to Praying God's Promises*. Every Home for Christ International, 2012.

Hagin, Kenneth. *The Believer's Authority*. Tulsa: Published by Kenneth Hagin Ministries, 1985.

Hamon, Bill. *Prophets and Personal Prophesy: God's Prophetic Voice Today*. Santa Rosa Beach: Destiny Image, 1993.

Kemp, Tony. *How to Partner with Angels to Usher in the Glory*. Quincy: Brewer Publishing, 1984.

Vallotton, Kris. *Basic Training for the Prophetic Ministry*. Shippensburg: Destiny Image, Publishers, Inc., 2005.

9 798887 380377